THE FURTHER EDUCATION

CURRICULUM

IN ENGLAND

An Introduction

by
Anna Frankel and Frank Reeves

**Bilston College Publications
in association with
Education Now**

Published 1996 by Bilston Community College Publications,
Bilston (EO & C) Training Ltd., Green Lanes, Wellington Road, Bilston,
Wolverhampton WV14 6EW, England, in association with
Education Now Publishing Co-operative Ltd
P.O.Box 186, Derby

British Cataloguing in Publication Data

Anna Frankel and Frank Reeves
    The Further Education Curriculum in England
    An Introduction
    1. Further Education 2. Curriculum 3. Socio-cultural aspects
    I Title II Frankel, Anna III Reeves, Frank
    370.1934

    ISBN 1-871526-19-1

Any opinions expressed are those of the authors. They should not be interpreted as representative of the views of Bilston Community College's corporation, corporation members, chief executive, or staff.

Design and production: Bilston Community College Publications
in association with Education Now Publishing Co-operative Ltd.

Printed by Mastaprint, Sandiacre, Nottinghamshire

CONTENTS

Acknowledgements

Our title was planned eighteen months ago as part of a series, but the urgent need for a concise, modern introduction to the further education curriculum was forcibly impressed on us when we attempted to explain the work of our college to visitors from the Community College Association of South Africa (CCASA). Our inspiration came from the enthusiasm of Dikeledi Molatoli, Martin Mulcahy, Flavia Monyemore, and Anthony Khatle, and their commitment to the life-long education of all the people of South Africa.

The authors, both senior managers expected to meet deadlines, achieve targets, and balance budgets in the course of their daily work in a busy community college, failed to keep to their writing schedule. Entreaties from Professor Roland Meighan of *Education Now* and threats from Susan Thompson and Claudette Hutchinson, managers of Bilston (E O & C) Training Ltd. (one of Bilston College's companies), eventually forced us to write against the clock at night and weekends for two months in January and February 1996. Fortunately, the weather was bad and the Chief Executive went on a business trip.

We acknowledge the contribution of the company progress-chasers to the book's production but must point out that it is impossible to write consistently and to our own academic standards under such working conditions. Readers will see that we needed more time. It is to be hoped, however, that what the book lacks in considered and researched academic argument, it makes up for in immediacy of expression. The authors are experiencing, like child birth, the emergence of the new further education curriculum at first hand, and describe the experience with all its pain and pleasure. These are patients', not doctors' observations.

What is obvious to anyone studying further education is the relative scarcity of factual information and germane research. In writing about the further education curriculum, we feel unable to acknowledge debts other than to early pioneers such as A J Peters, L M Cantor and I F Roberts. The failure to fund a comprehensive programme of social scientific research into further education is, in our view, nothing short of a national scandal. The aim, as we see it, is to build a comprehensive student-centred curriculum, providing genuine equality of opportunity. But this will be achieved only by the development of sound educational practice, properly supported and based on research into the nature and effects of further education. The primary objective of such a research programme must be to discover the best way of creating a learning society for all sections of the population.

We should like to thank Keith Wymer, Bilston Community College's visionary chief executive, for his sound advice. We are grateful to Perminder Bains for her wizardry in word processing and formatting the manuscript, to Claudette Hutchinson for compiling the list of abbreviations, to Shirley McFarquhar, Barry Hutchinson, Lorayne Craig, and Natalie Spencer for key-boarding contributions, to Simon Grigg for the cover design, and to all at *Education Now* for their encouragement and publishing expertise - AF and FWR.

Chapter One

Introduction to the further education curriculum

Studying the curriculum

In the 17th century, the Latin word *curriculum*, translated as *race course* or *chariot*, was transposed to mean a *course,* then a *course of study* and, eventually, *a list of courses offered by an educational establishment* or, indeed, any *plan of activity.* Increasingly elaborate technical definitions of the curriculum have been developed in recent years by social scientists and educationalists studying the transmission process in educational institutions, mostly schools.

Jenkins and Shipman (1976, p.6), for example, define a curriculum as "the formulation and implementation of an educational proposal to be taught and learned within a school or other institution and for which the institution accepts responsibility at three levels, its rationale, its actual implementation, and its effects".

Michael Young describes the task of curriculum studies thus:

> Education is a selection and organisation from the available knowledge at a particular time which involves conscious or unconscious choices. It would seem that it is, or should be, the central task of the sociology of education to relate these principles of selection and organisation that underlie curricula to their institutional and interactional setting ... and to the wider social structure (Young, 1971, p. 14).

Basil Bernstein also emphasises the need to study curriculum in the context of the social structure, particularly of its power relations and in the maintenance of social control:

2 Introduction to the further education curriculum

> How a society selects, classifies, distributes, transmits, and evaluates the educational knowledge it considers to be public reflects both the distribution of power and the principles of social control (Bernstein, 1973, p. 227).

Denis Lawton distinguishes between a restricted meaning of curriculum as the official content of lessons and a broader definition as the learning which is planned or guided by an educational institution. He, too, sees this broader curriculum as "a selection from the culture of a society":

> Certain aspects of our way of life, certain kinds of knowledge, certain attitudes and values are regarded as so important that their transmission to the next generation is not left to chance in our society but is entrusted to specially-trained professionals (teachers) in elaborate and expensive institutions... (Lawton, 1975, pp. 6-7).

Lawton believes that until 1944 there were two very different kinds of selection from British culture: "high status knowledge plus a certain kind of character training for the future leaders of society, in public and grammar schools; low-status, *elementary* practical skills, and training for obedience and conformity for the future *lower orders*" (p.8). The question that needed to be addressed was what kind of selection from culture was appropriate to create a secondary education for all.

To establish a relationship with this book's purpose, a series of similar questions needs to be addressed. What particular elements of culture - knowledge and beliefs, competence and skills, norms and values - have been selected and assembled to constitute the contemporary further education curriculum? What are the principles, values, or assumptions underlying their selection and assembly? What forces are at work changing the further education curriculum (the selection from culture)? And can the direction of change be discerned and the future curriculum predicted? What selection of culture is appropriate to create a further education for all?

The study of the curriculum may provide an exciting insight into something only reluctantly acknowledged in official or public circles, but quite obvious: that the knowledge, skills, and values considered important and worthy of formal educational transmission vary over time and location. It might be claimed that curriculum analysis, more than any other form of cultural studies, is capable of revealing the fundamental values of the society and age.

Questions of cause and effect are also important but difficult to disentangle and answer. To what extent are broader social forces fashioning the curriculum, and is the present curriculum affecting individual and group behaviour as well as national performance for many years to come? It is, of course, widely believed that national economic success is dependent on the knowledge and skill levels of the workforce - to which further education is seen as making an important contribution. But it is also plausible to argue that national education achievement is a product of economic success.

While Young, Bernstein, and Lawton provide a sound and exciting agenda, the study of the curriculum - or, as it is described above, the selection of the *representative* ideas of an age and place - raises complex methodological problems. Particularly apparent is the tendency for the concept of curriculum to expand inclusively to cover not only the statement of curriculum aims and course content, but descriptions of institutional rules, regulations, funding arrangements, learner responses to the curriculum, and outcomes intended and unintended, and for all discussion of cause and effect to become confused, diffuse, and inconclusive.

Features frequently highlighted in accounts of educational curricula include:

- course or content of study - *what?*

- aims, objectives, and rationale - *why?*

- user groups - *a curriculum for whom?*

- funders and providers - *how paid for?*

- accreditation - *by whom?*

- duration, timing, and modes of attendance - *when?*

- forms of transaction (e.g. teaching, learning methods, and assessment) - *how?*

- outcomes (e.g. acquired knowledge, skills, or values) - *to what effect?*

4   Introduction to the further education curriculum

- the direction of change - *where to?*

To provide an account of the selection and assembly of knowledge constituting the further education curriculum, each of these points will be expanded. Other aspects of the curriculum might have been included, such as the issue of location and accommodation (*where?*) and a description of lecturing staff (*taught by whom?*), but they are omitted from the book for reasons of space and concision. What follows is, in effect, an account of certain features of the curriculum of English further education with a focus on its definition, content, rationale, user groups, providers, accrediting bodies, modes of delivery, and outcomes. The primary aim is to provide a description of its more salient features, but there is a tendency to explain the curriculum historically and, in places, to evaluate it critically and to predict its future development.

Introducing the further education curriculum

This chapter defines *further education* by referring to the work of colleges and the various statutory frameworks in which they have had to operate. The further education curriculum, it is argued, may be conceived as a residue remaining after the extraction of other more dominant curricula.

Chapter Two addresses the issue of the content of the curriculum, distinguishing seven traditional elements: technical or vocational education, occupational training, general education, remedial and compensatory education, preparation for higher education, adult continuing education, and higher education, all of which contribute to the content of further education. Thus constituted, the further education curriculum is dissociative, multiform, or heterogeneous - a point readily conceded by many working in further education - but there are other features of further education such as voluntary attendance, competence-based approaches, and a funding methodology, which may be creating a more unified form of provision.

Chapter Three deals with aims, objectives, and rationale. What are the reasons given by the government and other powerful bodies for supporting and funding the further education sector at public expense? Traditionally, these may be summarised as education for work, citizenship, recreation, culture, and social mobility. Recently, the government has become fixated, to the exclusion of much else, on further education as a tool of national economic regeneration. To this end, it has given its support to a National Council for Vocational Qualifications and a set of National Targets for Education and Training, with employers playing a leading role in steering the vocational curriculum and the strategy of colleges. In contrast, the European Commission's view is based on a broader concept of preparing the whole population - not just the work force - for the *learning society*.

Chapter Four focuses on the users of further education - who they are, what they expect from further education, and how the curriculum has been adapted to their needs. The social categories of social class, age, gender, race, and disability, are each examined to assess the degree of responsiveness of the curriculum to the perceived needs of user groups.

Chapter Five describes the changes to the methods of funding and providing further education since 1944, and the way respective funding regimes have impacted upon the curriculum. In particular, the chapter dwells on the effect the Further Education Funding Council's funding methodology has had upon college provision and the resourcing of programmes. Its aim is to expand participation in further education at minimum cost. Many features of the college curriculum may be seen as cost-saving measures adapted for education from the modern world of business. Indeed, the metaphor of the *educational supermarket* seems aptly to apply to the new further education curriculum.

Chapter Six deals with the accreditation of the further education curriculum. In further education, the function of setting examinations and granting awards is separated institutionally from the function of course provision, teaching, and learning. Awarding bodies compete with one another in marketing their awards, while students' acquisition of awards is treated as a measure of performance for college funding and quality assurance purposes. The situation is immensely complex: for vocational education alone, the list of qualifications approved for further education includes 159 awarding bodies and 2000 qualifications.

Chapter Seven describes the time sequences of further education, the duration and timing of its courses, and the common attendance modes. Time is one of the most important aspects of the further education curriculum, and there is an increasing realisation that time is money. The chapter is devoted to a discussion of further education's six time cycles: the awards cycle, the student cycle, the industrial cycle, the teacher cycle, the funding cycle, and the benefits cycle.

Chapter Eight provides an account of the forms of transaction between teachers and learners in further education. It focuses on what learners do to learn and what teachers do when working with learners. It deals with teaching methods, classroom and workshop-based teaching, flexible and open learning, the use of information technology, accreditation of prior learning, which students are successful, and how students prefer to learn.

Chapter Nine assesses the outcome of further education. What effect does the further education curriculum actually have on students, employers, and society generally? Outcomes are reviewed in terms of government performance indicators, qualifications, success in obtaining employment, definitions of progression, increasing skills, and student satisfaction. The question is raised as to whether the aim of further education after all should be to improve people's education which, of course, is not the same thing as making them more qualified or helping them to acquire skills. The main outcome of further education may not be education at all, but an increase in counselling, confidence-raising, occupational therapy, and certification.

Chapter Ten serves as a conclusion. It draws out the main factors transforming the face of further education, such as the drive for mass provision and equality of opportunity. It discusses educational partnerships, organisational systems, student progression, accreditation, competence, learning-centredness, staff specialisation, educational products and packages, and automation. Operating simultaneously, these features are determining the direction of curriculum change in further education.

Defining further education

Further education, a particularly ambiguous term, whose connotation and denotation have varied considerably in the last hundred years, must first be defined. Situated in the social structure somewhere between the compulsory school sector on the one hand and industry and higher education on the other, further education is also an obvious candidate for an analysis - along Bernsteinian lines - of the way its curriculum has been selected, classified, and distributed by political, economic, and technical interest groups.

What comprises further education in England and Wales? The term *further education* was used and popularised in the Ministry of Education's *Pamphlet number 8* (1947), dealing with the scope and content of further education opportunities under the 1944 Education Act. The question has been answered in a number of different ways with a series of statutory definitions being devised by governments to accommodate, or contain, a reality that has evolved organically in response to national, regional, and local user needs and funding availability.

Text-book definitions

Peters.   Peters (1967, p.1) pointed out that *further education* could be used in a wide sense to mean "any education undergone by someone who has left school, whether in a definite institution or organised course, by self-directed study, or merely through life itself". He confined himself, however, to dealing with its statutory meaning which, under Section 41 of the 1944 Education Act, consisted of "full-time and part-time education for persons over compulsory school age" as well as "leisure-time occupation, in such organised cultural training and recreative activities as are suited to [the] requirements [of] persons over compulsory school age who are able and willing to profit" (p.2). In broad terms, further education then included full and part-time general education and vocational training as well as (non-vocational) social and recreational education provision. It excluded post-compulsory-school-age secondary-school education, teacher training, and university education. Peters noted that there was no clear boundary between further education and industrial or works training (provided usually by an employer at a place of work).

Cantor and Roberts.   In their popular text (1986, p.260), Cantor and Roberts defined *further education* in curriculum terms as comprising "all forms of post-school education except the universities".   It was "broadly vocational in purpose" but also included "provision for continued general education and for cultural and leisure activities". They distinguished between advanced and non-advanced further education, the latter consisting of courses to BTEC National Certificate and Diploma and GCE A level and including City and Guilds, Royal Society of Arts, and Regional Examination Board qualifications. Much of advanced higher education has since transferred with the polytechnics - now universities - to the higher education sector.

Statutory definitions

The Education Act, 1944.   Fifty years ago, Section 41 of the 1944 Education Act defined *further education* as full-time and part-time education and leisure-time involvement in organised cultural training and recreative activities for persons over compulsory school age.   But even pupils below this age could engage in further education if the provision was part of a *scheme* of further education, and pupils above this age might remain in secondary education if this was part of a secondary education *plan*. School pupils were not excluded from further education if it were regarded as suitable for them: further education was not statutorily age-related as - at least for funding purposes - it has now become. Further education was also clearly conceived not only as study orientated to work and/or undertaken in working time, but as non-vocational education orientated to leisure-time pursuits and/or undertaken in leisure time.

While the higher education work of universities would have been excluded in 1944 as beyond the ambit of the Education Ministry, the higher education courses undertaken in technical colleges - if not validated by them - formed an important part of further education. The 1944 definition accommodated the reality of the overlapping boundaries between, and local variation in, the respective scope of secondary, further, and higher education.

The Education Reform Act, 1988. The Education Reform Act continued to define further education as full-time and part-time education for persons over compulsory school age (including vocational, social, physical and recreational training) together with organised leisure-time occupation provided in connection with the provision of such education (section 120). But the Act achieved a much more restricted definition by specifying what local authorities were permitted to fund in the new further education schemes they were obliged to draw up.

Local authorities were no longer expected to fund polytechnic *advanced further* (higher) education. All first and higher degree courses leading to qualifications of the Council for National Academic Awards (CNAA) qualifications, polytechnics, and universities, all full-time Diplomas of Higher Education and BTEC Higher National Diplomas, initial teacher training courses and full-time in-service teacher training courses of more than a year's duration were removed from local authority responsibility, leaving local authorities with the residue of non-advanced further education. But local authorities retained powers to fund further education colleges for higher education qualifications given by professional bodies and for part-time courses leading to Higher National qualifications and Diplomas of Higher Education.

In addition, local authorities were no longer allowed to fund directly college facilities for students under compulsory school age, and indeed over that age, remaining in school sixth forms. For funding purposes, the new definition of further education excluded full-time higher education and pre-16 and post-16 school provision.

This did not mean that full-time higher education and courses for school-based groups ceased to exist in further education colleges, but only that it could no longer be local authority funded. Some work funded from other sources (fees from employers or students and transfer payments by universities or schools) did continue, but on a smaller scale. The Education Reform Act resulted, then, in a much more rigid institutional separation of further education from higher education on the one hand and school-based provision on the other.

The Further and Higher Education Act, 1992. Since 1992, with the passing of the Further and Higher Education Act, the term *further education* has acquired an essentially new and curtailed statutory definition setting out its function, its position in relation to the national education system as a whole, when and how it may take place, and the kinds of institution providing it. Superimposed deliberately upon earlier traditional connotations, *further education* now refers to full-time and part-time vocational, social, physical, and recreational education and training for persons over compulsory school age (and any leisure activities which form part of that provision).

By specifying what courses may be funded by the Further Education Funding Council (set up in 1992), Schedule 2 of the Further and Higher Education Act creates an even more explicit official definition of further education. It is conceived collectively as consisting of courses that lead to vocational qualifications, courses aimed at achieving academic qualifications for entry into higher education, courses to prepare students for further education, and courses in basic literacy and numeracy, in English for speakers of other languages, and in independent living skills for persons with learning difficulties. A notable exclusion for funding purposes is a major area of traditional further education: non-vocational adult continuing education. It remains a bone of popular contention as to whether courses recognised for so long as an integral part of the further education family should be excluded from funding on the basis that they have no formal qualification aims.

In regard to its institutional setting, further education comprises education undertaken in general further education colleges, sixth-form colleges, tertiary colleges, agricultural, horticultural, art and design, and performing arts colleges and certain other specialist adult colleges, all offering specific vocational training or general education courses.

Some of the terms used here may need brief explanation. A general *further education college* offers a variety of different full and part-time technical, vocational, and general academic education courses for 16-to-19-year olds and adults, many of them in work or seeking it. A *sixth-form college* has traditionally provided one or two-year, mainly full-time academic courses for 16-to-19 year olds. A *tertiary college*, often combining further education, sixth-form and sixth-form college facilities in one institution, aims to provide for the education and training requirements of the majority of 16-to-19-year olds and adults living in a given locality. *Adult colleges*, not mentioned in the above list, because most are still run by local education authorities and are not part of the statutory further education sector, have traditionally offered recreational or non-vocational, mainly part-time evening courses, to adults, but in recent years there has been diversification into academic courses and basic education. Some further education and tertiary colleges have been titled *community colleges*. This usually implies that they provide a service for a wide section of the population of a locality, often on an outreach and partnership basis, and offer a comprehensive range of full or part-time technical and general education courses, both vocational and non-vocational, thus undertaking the additional function of an adult college.

The new further education specifically excludes secondary education - the education available in (the sixth forms of) schools for 16-to-18-year olds who have completed compulsory schooling. Most higher education has also been excluded, except higher national certificates and some part-time professional qualifications (so-called *non-prescribed* higher education). Despite the elevation of the polytechnics (which provided most of what was known as *advanced* further education) to university status, a final unambiguous institutional separation of advanced from non-advanced courses of study remains illusive. Demarcation issues also continue to be posed by questions of payment for, and provision of, industrial training for employed and unemployed people.

The definition and the institutional basis of the broad category now known as further and adult continuing education has developed steadily in the last one hundred years in response to the changing social and economic structure and the perceived needs and demands of emergent social groups. The 1992 Act, however, has altered in radical fashion earlier more expansive concepts of further education.

It has been observed that further education prior to 1992 may have been defined less restrictively but the availability of public funds was unrelated to demand with the consequence that educational needs remained unsatisfied. The irony is that a more restrictive definition of further education means that needs may now be satisfied provided that they meet the strict funding criteria - a significant and controversial provision.

While the 1992 statutory definition of further education must serve to focus study of the further education curriculum, it is important to acknowledge broader traditions, their cross-fertilisation, continuing evolution and tension, and unresolved demarcations in the sector as a whole.   Conversely, the wide range of institutions comprising the sector and some of the specialist curricula they offer (e.g. that of sixth-form colleges) renders the notion of a national further education curriculum somewhat of an abstraction.   It is for these reasons that this study tends to focus on the curriculum of the traditional general further education college, rather than on that of sixth-form colleges, or specialist agricultural, or art and design, colleges.   But even for further education colleges, the wide-ranging needs of the students, employers and other users, and the diversity of the sector's response to them makes it difficult to talk of a single further education curriculum.   Further education has been conceived as an untidy *residue* of the curricula of other institutions, but it is more accurately described, as in the next chapter, as a *dissociative* curriculum.

Further education as residue

The statutory definitions of further education mentioned above are evidence that further education has long been conceived in government and academic circles as a *residue* remaining after the extraction of school and university education on the one hand and work-based training on the other.   Further education has been conceived and developed as a *residual* or *other* category in a number of different senses.

Residue of school general education.   The progressive raising of the school leaving age, the division of elementary education into primary and secondary sectors, the consolidation of the secondary education sector and the development of sixth-forms in comprehensive secondary schools, have transferred the main responsibility for the continuing education of young people to the schools (with reduced exposure to the technical and practical components of the further education curriculum). Further education has long been expected to furnish general education for those over compulsory school age who missed out or failed to achieve a sufficiently high standard at school. Thus schools are the primary providers of general education with further education filling any remaining need.

Residue of higher education.   The growth of the technical colleges and their successive transfer in waves to the higher education sector, accompanied by a focus on higher level work and full-time modes of attendance, have assisted the growth of applied courses in higher education but narrowed the range of levels of work in the remaining further education colleges.   Further education offers an important alternative or second-chance route into higher education for young people, and for adults not in sixth-forms or unable to study on a full-time basis.   It also continues to make available forms of higher education - often vocationally orientated - for those without access to traditional universities.   Further education still meets higher education need unmet by the universities.

Residue of industrial training.   In the 1980s, the Conservative government's insistence that relevant industrial and commercial training could be more effectively and efficiently directed and delivered by industry itself, in-company, by private training agencies, and by Training and Enterprise Councils, challenged the traditional raison d'être of the further education colleges.   This occurred against a backcloth of a general recession, a decline of manufacturing industry, a fall in the number of apprenticeships, and a massive growth in the number cf unemployed young people and adults.   Further education has continued to respond to employers' needs by offering preparatory and continuing technical training which, for reasons of effectiveness and efficiency, is not provided in-company.   Further education has also taken on the originally residually-conceived role of providing for large numbers of unemployed young people and adults, many with learning difficulties and disabilities, all of whom are likely to experience intense competition in attempting to enter the labour market.   Further education meets needs for training unmet by industry and training agencies.

The non-vocational, community residue.   The latest attempt to separate non-vocational adult continuing education from courses with technical, academic, and basic-education qualification aims, is a further example of *residual* thinking: adult continuing education has itself become a residue of the further education residue. While considered peripheral in most government thinking on education, the self-expressive character of a non-vocational education, serving community demand and rooted in popular culture is of crucial importance to increasing the general participation in, and personal relevance of, education. Conceptually, a local non-vocational *community* education represents the antithesis of education as induction to *high culture* or as preparation for employment. There are few signs that this residue will be absorbed into other sectors of education or that poorer people will afford to pay privately for non-vocational provision. Funding regulations now prevent further education from satisfying the widespread demand for non-vocational education.

There are, problems however, in describing the further education curriculum simply as *residue*. Further education colleges have been in existence since the middle of the 19th century and, while they have often performed functions undertaken by other institutions, they have sustained their own aims, courses, and approaches to education and training.

In common with cultural anthropology, curriculum studies has made use of different explanations of cultural (curriculum) change and development. A *diffusionist* curriculum theory assumes that a curriculum is created in one institution and spreads to others because of the power and influence of its advocates or its intrinsic usefulness, but it is equally possible that people may simultaneously invent and adopt the same practices because they have a common problem to solve. This represents a theory of *convergent invention.*

The contention of this book is that further education colleges have long been an important but neglected part of a broader, evolving system of universal education for young people and adults. Sharing a unity of purpose, however, colleges have developed their own selection of knowledge, skills, and values and presentation methods - a unique and distinctive *cultural pattern* - which deserves the title of the *further education curriculum.*

Chapter Two

The content of the further education curriculum
- *what?*

In their definition of further education given in Chapter One, Cantor and Roberts (1986) mention the broadly vocational nature of further education. That chapter also showed that further education had accumulated residues of school, higher, and adult education, and industrial training, each with its own curriculum traditions. Educational institutions have often been able to fulfil the demands made upon them by offering a more or less integrated curriculum provision, but the requirements on further education to meet the demands of different user groups have been so disparate that, while some kind of integrative process might be discernible, it is difficult to demonstrate the existence of a single distinctive curriculum for further education. Although perhaps an aspiration, it is not a unitary reality in the same way as is the curriculum of the secondary school or even the curriculum of the university sector.

The further education curriculum is best described as *dissociative, multiform,* or *heterogeneous,* a federation of curricula, drawing on a variety of different educational traditions. To describe such a curriculum requires an analysis of each of the recognised constituent elements as well as an account of the kinds of relationship that bind them together to produce what is recognisably further education. This chapter lists, first, the elements or building blocks and then the relational features or mortar which, all together, create the further education phenomenon.

Seven dissociative elements

From the definitions so far given, a number of traditional elements of the further education curriculum may be identified:

- technical or vocational education.

- occupational training.
- general education.
- remedial and compensatory education.
- preparation for higher education.
- adult continuing education.
- higher education.

Of these, technical and vocational education and, to some extent, adult continuing education, have traditionally been regarded as quintessential to further education, but their delivery has always required a foundation of general education and, in its absence, remedial and compensatory measures.

Technical or vocational education

Derived from a Greek root meaning *art* or *craft*, the adjective *technical* has come to describe the characteristics of arts and sciences, in particular of mechanical arts and applied sciences, and of skilled occupations and professions. The technical dimension of a subject relates closely to the study of the practical and ordered means of successfully undertaking a task, as distinct from a mere general appreciation of its effects and implications. Technical education involves preparation of individuals to undertake occupations requiring various kinds and degrees of knowledge and skill. There is a wide range of education for technical ability, traditionally described, in ascending order of theoretical content as provision for operatives, craftsmen, technicians, and technologists. Vocational education, now frequently used conterminously with technical education, still carries an older connotation of a *calling*, or, more typically, a lifelong career or professional commitment.

Technical and vocational education has usually involved a programme of study with a component of theoretical knowledge, as well as of practical skill acquisition, as preparation for a professional or skilled occupation involving autonomous working. It has traditionally consisted of preparatory study in a classroom, studio, laboratory, or training workshop, prior to, or in parallel with, full or partial performance on the job. The paradigm is that of preparation for the professions or for skilled arts and crafts.

Public funding for technical education became available after the Technical Instruction Act of 1889. Fleshing out the implications of the 1944 Education Act, the Ministry of Education pamphlet on further education (8, 1947) contained brief descriptions of technical education and qualifications available in six broad occupational groupings: agricultural and associated, building and associated, chemical manufacture and process, commerce, engineering and related, and other industries (25 listed) (p.332). Further education, according to Crowther, has grown up as the handmaiden of employment (Ministry of Education, 1959, p.333). An extreme and probably mistaken view frequently expressed is that the further education curriculum is not a product of educational policy at all, but of employer need.

A technical or further education college typically offered a range of occupational qualifications to meet the multiple demands of the local economy it served, although in some areas where single industries predominated, a college might develop a specialism, such as heavy engineering, that overshadowed its other provision. Nevertheless, the colleges in the sector are now generally polytechnical in nature, although this has not always been the case, and exceptions remain in the form of agricultural and horticultural colleges, and colleges of art and design, dance, and music. A number of colleges, formerly specialising in subjects such as commerce, building, or art, have either broadened the occupational range of their curriculum or have been amalgamated to become faculties of larger institutions.

The traditional technical and vocational curriculum of further education is revealed in the large number of occupational qualifications on offer, especially, for example, those validated by the Business and Technology Education Council (BTEC), the Royal Society of Arts (RSA), and the City and Guilds of London Institute (CGLI).

Occupational training

In contrast with traditional technical and vocational education, occupational training is the term used to describe learning by doing, often on the job itself, in the workshop or factory, by *watching Joe* or *sitting by Nellie*.

Training has traditionally referred to the acquisition of immediately practical skills, by imitation or repetition and, unlike education, is felt to lack the connotation of reflective or critical thinking. After elementary school, the vast majority of working people would have received no formal off-the-job training: if it were considered necessary, it occurred on the job through apprenticeship or other forms of learning from fellow workers. The Carr Report (HMSO, 1958) recommended that industrial training remain the responsibility of industry.

The growth of off-the-job training for craftsmen and operatives assisted by the 1964 Industrial Training Act, resulted in the expansion of both education and training and an erosion of earlier distinctions between technical and vocational education on the one hand and occupational training on the other. The use of the higher status term *education* is now extended to describe occupational education and training as a whole, with the implication that preparation for a profession or career is taking place - clearly a moot point in a context of high levels of unemployment and arguments about deskilling versus upskilling. Since the 19th century, technical colleges have played a part in social-class transformation and mobility by providing courses ranging from very basic to post-graduate levels to meet the changing demand for skilled labour. College-based provision for unemployed people, supported in the 1980s by the Manpower Services Commission (created by the Employment and Training Act, 1973), has raised important questions about the nature, purpose, and location of training.

General education

Further education has also provided a general education, a necessary foundation on which to develop applied technical knowledge and skills, but its role has changed with the growth and effectiveness, first of elementary education, and then of secondary schooling, against a background of the successive raising of the school leaving age.

Initially, working-class educational levels were so low that it was impractical to separate general and technical education, the former having to support the latter, and each contributing to improved performance in employment. Introducing the Elementary Education Bill in 1870, W. E. Forster observed that "upon the speedy provision of elementary education depends our industrial prosperity. It is of no use trying to give technical teaching to our artizans without elementary education" (Maclure, 1973, pp.104-5).

In 1870, while schooling was not compulsory, elementary education was made available up to the age of 12 and, by 1876, 50 per cent of the 5 to 13 age group were receiving compulsory education under the School Boards. The 1880 Mundella Act made education compulsory between the ages of 5 to 10. In 1918, the school leaving age was raised to 14 and in 1947, after postponement due to war, to 15. It was raised to 16 in 1972-3.

To qualify for a grant from the LEA, a school had to meet a criterion of eligibility. The requirement that a secondary school must provide a general education - physical, mental, and moral - was set out in the 1904 Regulations for Secondary Schools. They determined that the curriculum for all secondary schools would be modelled on that of the grammar and public schools, thus isolating secondary education for 80 years from the ideas and influences of technical education.

Secondary schools, of course, remain the primary providers of general education for young people, but the colleges continue to offer the General Certificate of Secondary Education (GCSE) in a variety of subjects both for young adults, who after leaving school wish to improve or extend their performance, and for adults wishing to return to study.

The emphasis placed on general education has varied historically from college to college, with some developing a strong liberal arts ethos, while others focused on practical bread-and-butter skills. General education has often been supported by the size and strength of a college's adult continuing education work, with some of the colleges in the sector being founded on this tradition. Worth mentioning in this respect are the residential colleges of adult education such as Ruskin, Fircroft, and Colleg Harlech, which originally provided full-time residential courses lasting one or two years in social studies for working people.

Impetus to the general education tradition in further education was added by the reorganisation in the 1970s, in some areas, of further education colleges, school sixth-forms, sixth-form centres, and adult education, into tertiary colleges, providing academic and technical courses for all 16-to-19 year-olds and adults.

Remedial and compensatory education

In recognition of students' widely varying levels of preparedness for study, most colleges now provide a range of preparatory, compensatory, and remedial courses, including programmes in literacy and numeracy and support for students with learning difficulties and disabilities. The Crowther Report (Ministry of Education, 1959) observed that "the maintenance of the basic educational skills of ability to read, write and calculate correctly is for backward boys and girls a quite essential part of vocational training as well as of general education. Because they learn slowly, and think and write and read slowly, this side of their county college training is likely to take as much of the available time as the teaching of vocational subjects to abler boys and girls" (pp.178-9).

Today, adult sections of the population, who would never previously have considered it feasible to undertake study, are now, after experience of unemployment, childcare, debilitative illness, or disability, entering further education in the belief that the qualifications gained there will help their entry to the labour market.

The preparatory, compensatory, and remedial work of colleges is frequently classified into four categories: basic skills, English (for speakers of other languages), provision for people with learning difficulties and/or disabilities, and additional support.

Basic skills are defined as "the ability to read, write, and speak in English and use mathematics at a level necessary to function and progress at work and in society in general".   According to the Adult Literacy and Basic Skills Unit (ALBSU), now known as the Basic Skills Agency (BSA), basic skills provision is necessary for young people and adults who can hardly read, or who have such limited reading skills that they can understand only simple information, or who can read but find writing and spelling difficult, or who have difficulty with number work and have no mathematical qualifications, or whose first language is not English and who need English tuition.   This last provision is also known as *English for Speakers of Other Languages* (ESOL).   It is estimated that 13 per cent of adults, or six million people, in the United Kingdom have problems with reading, writing or basic mathematics (ALBSU, 1992).

Colleges also provide programmes in independent living and communication *for individuals with learning difficulties and/or disabilities* (often referred to as *special needs* programmes).   There is an immense range of individual need but, while colleges recognise the diversity of this particular student population, their work is frequently categorised into provision for four groups: physical disability (including sensory), mental handicap, mental illness, and behavioural difficulty (see Chapter Four).   Some institutions provide specialist facilities for particular groups such as the hearing impaired, or the blind or partially sighted.   Various schemes for disruptive pupils have been developed jointly with schools and, in liaison with the probation service, work has been undertaken with young offenders.   Some further education colleges have a tradition of working on an outreach basis in prisons. Other outreach projects with organisations such as the health service, local authority day centres, Cheshire homes, and MIND increase the availability of further education.

Under college funding methodology, extra funds can be claimed for *additional support* given to a student to help her gain access to, progress towards, or achieve her learning goals, whether the need arises from a language or learning difficulty or disability. Colleges may also help disabled students by providing personal assistance, individual tuition, and special equipment.

Preparation for higher education

General education may assist students in obtaining work, in gaining technical qualifications, or in helping students complete courses to qualify them for entry to higher education institutions. With nearly a third of young people now undertaking higher education courses, preparation for entry into university is another important element of the further education curriculum, represented by GCE Advanced level programmes and accredited *Access into Higher Education* courses.

Further education colleges have traditionally provided a route (sometimes the only available route) into higher education for those leaving school at 16 (formerly 15) and for adult returners, a role statutorily recognised in schedule 2 of the Further and Higher Education Act. The new centrally-funded sector created by the Act now includes well over 100 specialist sixth-form colleges, most of whose business is to provide GCE A level courses to prepare students for university entry.

Adult continuing education

Many further education colleges also provide day and evening classes in cultural and recreative subjects, for employed, unemployed, and retired adults, although some local authorities have developed separate free-standing adult education centres. This element of the curriculum is usually referred to as *non-vocational,* or *adult continuing education.* Evening courses in art and craft, which traditionally would be studied for expressive purposes and not for a qualification, might be regarded as the paradigm of this element of the curriculum, but many of the courses offered by adult education services and institutions are, in fact, general, remedial, or preparatory for further study. In 1993 there were 1,400,000 FE enrolments in Adult Education Centres, two thirds in the evening, and three quarters were female students (DFE, 1995). The distinction between vocational, technical, and non-vocational education (the last officially labelled *adult education*) was created in 1924 when the conditions of grant aid for the general and non-vocational education of adults were first issued as separate regulations.

Contrary to popular stereotype, by 1994, the great majority of students in the further education sector was adult. With large numbers of adult students unemployed and studying for vocational qualifications or entry into higher education, and the development of the concepts of lifelong learning, adult training, and professional updating, the distinction between *vocational* preparation courses for younger age groups and recreative *non-vocational* courses for adults (together with the label, *adult continuing education*) has become increasingly untenable.

Higher education

A number of further education colleges run higher education programmes, preparing for degrees, Higher National Certificate and Diploma courses, and higher professional qualifications in areas such as personnel management and social work. Further education has traditionally extended its provision by offering advanced courses, but larger, more successful colleges, with the greatest concentration of advanced work, have periodically detached themselves from their base, shedding lower level courses and part-time students, to rise into the stratosphere of the university sector.

Following the Haldane Report of 1906, the Royal College of Science and Royal School of Mines (founded after the Great Exhibition) and the Central Technical College (founded by the City and Guilds of London Institute in 1884) were granted a Royal Charter in 1907 to become the Imperial College of Science and Technology of the University of London. The 1956 white paper *Technical Education* proposed the development of higher education to university level outside of the universities in nine (later ten) Colleges of Advanced Technology, which, after Robbins (HMSO, 1963) were upgraded to university status. The Robbins Report on Higher Education (HMSO, 1963) also proposed the Council for National Academic Awards (CNAA) be given a royal charter to grant degrees in all fields of study. The 1966 white paper *A Plan for Polytechnics and Other Colleges* (HMSO, 1966) recommended the incorporation of some sixty colleges of technology, building, art, and commerce into 30 new polytechnics which, by 1992, had assumed the title of university and were funded alongside the traditional universities. Robinson (1968) gives a fascinating account of the escapology of the larger technical colleges into higher education.

The distinction between further and higher education courses has always been difficult to make. The further education sector continues to provide advanced courses of a technical or applied nature. In November 1993, 7 per cent of students were on higher education courses (DFE, 1995). In recent years, universities have increasingly entered into arrangements to give accreditation for higher level courses offered, in whole or in part, by further education colleges. The essential difference between the curriculum of universities and of further education, however, is that the former institutions are self-validating - awarding their own degrees and other qualifications - while the colleges are dependent on external validation (see below).

Dissociation of course accreditation and course provision

Further education has its origins in Victorian philanthropic voluntary foundations, supported and extended by various cautious governmental interventions that allowed local authorities to raise public funds to support the provision of technical instruction.   The long-standing division in further education between the setting of syllabuses and examinations on the one hand and the formation and teaching of courses of instruction to prepare students for examinations on the other hand was also laid in the 19th century. In non-advanced further education, the tradition survives of state-funded college providers of courses entering students for examinations set by private examination boards.

With the acquisition of the power to award officially recognised qualifications to their own students, the polytechnics, as new universities, have striven and succeeded, for what used to be known as *advanced further education*, in bridging this historical division of responsibility.   The separation of the business of devising and accrediting the curriculum from that of teaching it, however, remains engrained in further education, together with the distinction between examination fees and accreditation costs on the one hand and course fees and the costs of course provision on the other.

This is another reason for the further education curriculum's dissociative form, with colleges selecting various syllabuses from the portfolios of a number of nationally-recognised private examination boards, each with its own rationale and autonomy. With the possible exception of non-vocational education, the college curriculum, therefore, does not spring organically from an expression or assessment of potential local user need and is, to a greater degree, pre-packaged, with disparate elements fitting uneasily together.

Associative characteristics

The seven elements described above contribute to the further education curriculum and many, if not all, will coexist in a typical further education college. This proximity within a common organisational framework, staffed by personnel working across discipline or accreditation areas, has led almost inevitably to the emergence of unifying and transformatory tendencies - a set of common causes, responses, effects, and outcomes. These might be termed the associative or bonding characteristics of the further education curriculum, some of the most obvious of which are listed below:

General

- voluntary attendance and need or demand orientation.
- tradition of recruiting and providing for students locally (not nationally).
- increasing majority of adult students.
- existence of a distinctive part-time attendance mode.
- multi-vocational or polytechnical provision.
- availability of NCVQ framework to assist the standardisation of curriculum approaches and levels.
- legacy of practical skill training manifested in fondness for behavioural objectives and competence-based approaches.
- growth of provision for the unemployed, challenging the viability of earlier distinctions between learning for work and for leisure.
- statutory duty to provide for people with learning difficulties and disabilities.

Organisational

- a statutory framework.
- nationally allocated funding and funding methodology based on student numbers and costs.
- common traditions and forms of organisation and management.

- similar conditions of service for staff.
- common facilities for students: teaching rooms, sports halls, canteens, child-care, etc.
- an integrated college marketing programme.

Most of these points are dealt with at greater length elsewhere in this book. Each has a unifying practical or ideological effect on the curriculum evolving within further education institutions.   For example, the application of the funding methodology is likely to standardise expenditure across curriculum areas and result in courses of similar length for similar qualifications.   If provision for the unemployed is to be effective, there must be closer co-ordination and greater integration of technical or vocational education, occupational training, general, adult, and remedial education, and preparation for higher education.

The further education curriculum is clearly in the process of rapid change. A leader in the *Times Educational Supplement* summed up the situation as follows:

> The idea that there is such a thing as an identifiable FE curriculum is a novel concept to some...
>
> Colleges are particularly well placed for curriculum development that could not only flesh out the vocational menu to educational advantage, but demonstrate how A level and General National Vocational Qualifications (GNVQ), for example, might overlap or merge... (*Times Educational Supplement*, 17.9.93).

The Association for Colleges, representing the interests of further education and other colleges in the sector, has given itself the task of leading the debate about the nature and purpose of post-16 education in order to create an independent and distinctive further education curriculum and a national framework (Association for Colleges, 1994). This book sets out some of the problems of achieving that independence and distinctiveness.

Chapter Three

The aims of the further education curriculum
- *why?*

What are the aims of the further education curriculum? What are colleges for? What do they set out to do? In one sense, the aims of further education consist in the purposes to which individual users put the service. These are many and varied but, when pressed, a majority of people is likely to claim that college attendance improves employment, promotion, or educational opportunities. In the main, people come to study to improve their future economic prospects. But there are many others who attend because they enjoy intellectual stimulation and the social life at college.

Most people who make use of the further education curriculum would not regard themselves as determining its content or method, even though their collective choices in the further education market might decide which courses a college continued to offer.   For the majority of students and staff, the curriculum is experienced as given.

This book, as a whole, describes the many different forces fashioning the further education curriculum. This chapter, however, attempts to summarise the justifications found in social policy since the middle of the 19th century for the public provision of further education. These justifications, representing the interests of informed and powerful groups, were widely articulated and, through careful balance and compromise, aggregated as the basis for successive government and local authority initiatives. They were the main reasons given for the public support for, and expenditure on, the further education curriculum. While a number of other justifications for the provision of further education was possible, none was repeated as frequently and to such effect as the generally-stated aims listed below, and none more than the economic justification. Consideration is also given in this chapter to the latest attempts at national and European level to develop and implement policy for the further education sector.

Education for work

Technical education.   The gradual realisation of the nation's need for technical education is exemplified by the development of a number of Victorian - mostly voluntary - institutions, important forerunners of today's further education.

In 1877, the London livery companies set up a committee to prepare a scheme for a system of technical education (City and Guilds, 1993, p.17). This became the City and Guilds of London Institute which aimed to provide "education adapted to the requirements of all classes of persons engaged, or preparing to engage in manufacturing or other industries". The Institute encouraged and subsidised evening classes for artisans and developed examinations in technical subjects.

The first polytechnic colleges (*polytechnic*, from the Greek, meaning *many arts*) were also set up at this time. One of the best known was founded by a Quinton Hogg and moved to premises in Regent Street in 1880. Hogg aimed at "the instruction of artisans and clerks in the principles and, to some extent, the practice of their bread winning pursuits" although classes were not to be designed or arranged "so as to be in substitution for the practical experience of the workshop or place of business but so as to be supplementary thereto" (Silver and Teague, 1977, p.17). Fees were low and the classes (run in collaboration with the recently formed City and Guilds of London Institute) included instruction in bricklaying, plumbing, electrical work, watch-making, photography, printing, and tailoring. Polytechnic foundations also developed secondary and technical schools and domestic science and trade classes which provided general education evening courses for persons engaged in work during the day, as well as day-time technical classes for more advanced students.

The Finsbury Technical College was opened in 1883 as a model trade school for the instruction of artisans and other persons preparing for intermediate posts in industrial works. Courses were held in the evening and day time and included not only mathematics and science but applied subjects such as building, engineering, and design.

Education for citizenship

In addition to preparing the population for work is the related task of educating them for a generally-conceived citizenship. The ideas of the right to a broad-based education or initiation as a citizen and of educating individuals to participate more fully and successfully in democratic society relate closely to the Owenite socialist ideal of the need for the working classes to achieve independence through co-operative effort.

The London Working Men's College, founded in 1854, offered liberal humanistic studies and education, through fellowship, to working men, with a curriculum by 1860-61, in descending order of popularity, of French, drawing, English grammar, Latin, book keeping, arithmetic, geometry, algebra, English composition, history of England, English literature, and geology (Harrison, 1954, p.59).   The college's founder, Frederick Maurice, aimed at giving freedom and order to the working class by liberating their minds (ibid., pp.24-5).

Ruskin College, founded in the university town of Oxford in 1899, was intended as a residential college for working men to enable them to achieve social change.   The curriculum focused neither on traditional university subjects such as divinity or classical languages, nor on occupational preparation, but on the social sciences (Pollins, 1984, pp.9-10).

The arguments and legislation for a broadly-based continuing education for citizenship - consisting of more than occupational training - came to the fore in and immediately after the First and Second World Wars when feelings of national solidarity and commonality of interest were ascendant.

Further education in the aftermath of wars.   Introducing the Education Bill in parliament in 1917, H A L Fisher, the President of the Board of Education, talked of the increased feeling of social solidarity created by the War:

> ... when you get a state of affairs under which the poor are asked to pour out their blood ... then every just mind begins to realise that the boundaries of citizenship are not determined by wealth, and that the same logic which leads us to desire an extension of the franchise points also to an extension of education ... industrial workers of the country are entitled to be considered primarily as citizens (*Hansard*, 10.8.1917, reproduced in Maclure, 1973, p.173).

Under the Fisher Act of 1918, local education authorities were given the duty of setting up day continuation schools to provide courses of study and instruction and physical training, without charging fees, for all young people up to the age of 16 (and after 7 years up to 18) and the power to oblige them to attend for 320 hours per year (Maclure, 1973, pp.171-2). The proposals were undermined by the depression, cuts imposed on government expenditure, and opposition from employers.   Few authorities used the power (only Rugby implemented the Act in full) and, by 1938, only about one fifth of elementary school leavers were receiving any kind of formal education and most of that through evening attendance.

In addition to raising the school leaving age to 15, the Education Act of 1944, revived the essential features of the Fisher Act in the form of *county colleges* to be established within three years to give part-time education in working hours to young persons up to the age of 18 for 330 hours per year. The provision was to be made compulsory on the four parties involved: young people, employers, local authorities and ministers, but once more, in the event, these clauses were never implemented because of the deteriorated economic situation.

The Ministry of Education (1947, pamphlet no. 8) explained the scope of the 1944 Act for further education as follows: "If a great extension of technical education is essential to the well-being of our economic life, so equally is a wide development of general adult education necessary if we are - as individuals or a nation - to deal competently and democratically with the complex political questions of our time". It is of considerable significance that neither the 1991 white paper nor the 1992 Further and Higher Education Act attach importance to education for citizenship.

Education for recreative and cultural pursuits

Coupled closely with the idea of educating the individual, not merely as a worker, but as an autonomous citizen, are the aims of providing for recreative and cultural interests. Often this is conceived in terms of gaining access to the prestigious and valued forms of liberal education available to the middle classes, but sometimes it is seen as a means of keeping working-class youngsters out of trouble. Crowther believed that the colleges in association with the youth service should assist young people in developing worthwhile leisure and recreational activities at a time "when many of them make a less worthwhile use of their free time than at any other period of their lives" (Ministry of Education, 1959, p.177).

The 1944 Education Act defined further education to include "leisure time occupation in ... organised cultural training and recreative activities". The Ministry of Education (1947, p.8) believed that as many people as possible should share in the appreciation of cultural achievements. Adult education has widely come to mean *non-vocational* education for people aged eighteen or more, and includes the provision of *liberal* education developed in the late nineteenth and early twentieth century and embodied in the network of adult education institutions, university extra-mural education, and Workers' Educational Association classes. (The WEA was founded in 1903.) The powers of various ministries before the Second World War to aid and establish community centres, village halls, playing fields, and other facilities for social and physical recreation were consolidated as part of the education service by the 1944 Education Act, and were at the time regarded as part of further education. Various other acts since then have determined expenditure in relation to such facilities, but in general the area has been underfunded and treated as non-essential.

The 1992 Act excludes non-vocational education (unless it is part of a vocational course) from the crucial Schedule 2 definition of further education for funding purposes and effectively deletes the recreational and cultural aim from the new further education sector - although *vocational* adult education courses in adult institutions can still be funded through partner institutions.

Education for social mobility, equality of opportunity, and equality

The aims of education for citizenship and of widening cultural and recreational horizons for working people are linked to a more fundamental concept of education as a significant means of increasing social mobility, opportunity, and equality, thereby contributing to social stability and the economic well-being and happiness of the population as a whole. Equal opportunity, interpreted in social-class terms, has been an objective of official educational policy since 1944 but, in reality, has come to mean increasing the upward flow of students (from working-class origins) through further education to employment or higher education - but not to creating a flow of students (from middle-class backgrounds) downwards (see Westergaard and Resler, 1975).

30 The aims of the further education curriculum

The expansion of further and higher education in the 1980s and 1990s is evidence of an unstated shift in aim and policy away from a selective approach to one of a mass system of open entry, in order to raise the education and training standards of the population as a whole. The official justification is in terms of national survival but expansion is also supported by those subscribing to greater equality and equality of opportunity for sections previously excluded by social class, gender, race and ethnicity, and disability.

The capacity of further education, in tandem with other sectors of education, to restructure wider social relations in either egalitarian or hierarchical ways is frequently assumed but seldom explicitly stated in official policy. Yet a wide range of social engineering projects may be inferred from the many public statements of educational intent.

For example, the Further Education Campaign Group of colleges launched a new manifesto in 1993 calling for "a single curriculum framework for post-16 education, embracing academic and vocational routes within a fully developed system of credit accumulation and transfer" (FECG, 1993, p.7). In a subsequent manifesto, the Association for Colleges (a new unitary organisation of colleges, replacing earlier associations including the Campaign Group) took up the quest for a single structure of qualifications "bringing academic and vocational courses within a common framework", to "provide parity of esteem for equal attainment regardless of subject area or intended destination" (AfC, 1995, May). The unitary curriculum framework is clearly intended to reduce wastage, increase choice, and improve equality of opportunity.

Serving the national economy by educating the workforce

A recurring theme in the history of further education is the claim that the British economy is under-performing in relation to other countries and the use of this assumption as a justification for increasing public funding and in government intervention in support of more technical education. This rationale for technical and further education is remarkably persistent and has been frequently restated, from the time of the Great Exhibition of 1851 onwards. W E Forster, introducing the Elementary Education Bill in 1870, argued that "if we leave our work folk any longer unskilled .... they will become overmatched in the competition of the world" (Maclure, 1973, pp.104-5).

In a speech made at Ruskin College, Oxford, in 1976, the Labour Prime Minister, James Callaghan, referred to the deficiencies in basic educational skills and the reluctance of the best students to enter industry. In 1982, his Conservative successor, Margaret Thatcher, announced the government's Technical and Vocational Educational Initiative - a five-year programme to be introduced, not by the Department of Education, but by the Manpower Services Commission, a branch of the Department of Employment, to develop general, technical, and vocational education for 14-to-18-year-olds. It was intended to provide a decisive orientation of the curriculum towards what was of immediate relevance "to the skills and know-how required by a technological society". By helping to equip young people with the skills employers were said to need, offering work experience, and developing "enterprise", it marked a significant departure from the earlier policy of offering only a general education in secondary schools.

In his foreword to the 1991 government white paper *Education and Training for the 21st Century*, John Major announced that there had been a revolution in Britain's education and training with the government's announcement of reforms backed by increased resources. The country was now building "the skilled and motivated workforce we need to take on international competition, and beat it". The white paper offered "the prospect of a workforce with first class skills to produce the wealth on which our society depends for its standard of living", (Vol. 1, p.64). The subsequent legislation of 1992 reinforced the almost exclusive focus of policy and funding on the *workforce* - not on the country's citizens in general. The 1995 *Competitiveness* White Paper reiterated the message: "To compete internationally the UK needs a highly motivated and well qualified work force... The Government's role is to help create the necessary conditions for this to happen" (ED, DFE, 1995, p.1).

National economic regeneration

Government, opposition, and business all agree that the further education curriculum has a key role in improving productivity and occupational skills to a level comparable with those of other advanced industrial countries. There is now a widespread acceptance that this must involve mass participation in education and training beyond compulsory school leaving age. The cost of an expanded provision, however, is considerable and necessitates priority being given to efficiency measures: educating and training more students or members of the workforce at a lower cost.

32   The aims of the further education curriculum

The government expects colleges to serve company training needs by providing employers with the range of courses they require. Individual students need to be given opportunities to acquire skills and qualifications of direct relevance to employment, while people displaced by economic or technological change, wishing to change career, or re-enter the labour market, should have a chance to retrain.   Colleges are seen as playing a key role in local economic development and regeneration.

The government's acknowledgement of the role of education and training in economic regeneration has now extended beyond exhortation to supporting two important initiatives aimed, first, at creating a national framework of occupational qualifications and, secondly, at using the framework as a means of setting attainment targets for training and education and then of measuring progress towards their achievement.   These are the National Vocational Qualification framework and the National Targets for Education and Training.

National Council for Vocational Qualifications

The recommendations of the Review of Vocational Qualifications (RVQ) Working Group set up in April 1985, under the chairship of H.G. DeVille, were accepted in the government White Paper *Working Together - Education and Training* of July 1986 (NCVQ, 1987a).   The National Council for Vocational Qualifications (NCVQ) was set up in the October of that year.   The NCVQ saw vocational qualifications - qualifications directly related to a person's competence in employment - as essential to the country's economic performance and to individual job satisfaction.

The tasks of NCVQ included securing standards of occupational competence through vocational qualifications and introducing a new national framework for vocational qualifications.   The Council did not itself intend to award qualifications, but to work with established examining bodies to introduce a simplified system of vocational qualifications based on employment-led standards of competence (NCVQ, 1987b).   The crude application of the competence approach to vocational qualifications has been criticised for de-emphasising and undermining the knowledge base of vocational education although the NCVQ has asserted that knowledge and understanding are integral to its concept of competence (but see Hyland, 1994).

In the general context of comparatively low levels of general education, questions have also been raised about the role and interest of employers in determining the vocational curriculum. The occupational areas covered include construction, extraction, land-based, engineering, manufacturing, transport, service, health, social care and protective service, business, and communication industries. A narrow, occupationally specific, instrumental, competence approach, eschewing knowledge, theory and general education might defeat the aim of producing a work force able to adapt to the rapidly changing requirements of the modern economy.

National Advisory Council for Education and Training Targets

The importance the government attached to the raising of the skill level of the nation's work force was demonstrated by the setting up of the National Training Task Force. In 1991, in partnership with industry and Trade Union Congress, the Task Force launched the *National Targets for Education and Training* (NTET) to raise standards of achievement in education and training. The aim was to secure "the competitiveness of the British economy and a higher standard of living for Britain's people" (DFE, 1992). The case for targets was stated unequivocally:

> Britain's trading position in a rapidly evolving world economy depends crucially on competitive skills. It is vital that we close the skills gap with our major competitors. Up-to-date skills are also essential to personal success at work.
>
> A quantum leap in foundation learning by young people and life-time learning is needed. That is why National Targets have been set to raise attainment in education and training.

The targets were of two kinds: foundation learning for young people, and life-time learning for the workforce as a whole. For example, 50 per cent of young people were required to reach NVQ level 3 or equivalent by the year 2000 while, by 1996, all employees were to take part in training or development activities.

In 1995, the National Advisory Council for Education and Training Targets updated the targets and published a review of progress and an action plan (NACETT, 1995). As a business-led body, it saw its main job as that of persuading employers to commit themselves to raising skill levels. Many employers apparently had still to acknowledge the link between training and industrial competitiveness.

An increase in participation rates in post-school education was a priority and employers had to be encouraged to provide training opportunities for their employees. Comparison with the country's major competitors showed there could be no room for complacency if the country were to improve its competitive position. Particular attention had to be given to securing a substantial increase in the number of young women achieving NVQs at level 3.

NCVQ and NTET serve as a stark revelation of the way the government has conceived and operationalised the purpose of education and training. An overwhelming emphasis is placed on the role of further education and higher education as a service to industry. The business interest is expected to play the leading role in setting educational objectives and defining the curriculum. The results are predictable. The competence, and output approaches have been criticised for reducing the curriculum to the testing of narrowly-defined, immediately specifiable and non-transferable behavioural skill objectives to the exclusion of a more general, knowledge-rich, and theoretically-sound approach. Can NVQs in their present form be the answer to the need for a flexible workforce if, as is generally agreed, the pace of economic change is accelerating so fast?

Europe and the learning society

The direction of further education is increasingly likely to be affected by the United Kingdom's membership of the European Community. A number of further education colleges are in receipt of funding from Europe for a wide variety of education and training programmes and there is pressure to maximise their contribution to the European vision.

The European Commission for Research, Education and Training (CRET) is concerned with the threats to the countries of Europe of increasing long-term unemployment and of social exclusion (particularly of young people). There is a recognition of the challenges of adjusting to the changing nature of work, the internationalisation of trade, and the arrival of *the information society*.

The Learning Society. According to the Commission, the information society, based on information technology, has resulted in both new opportunities for people to access knowledge, and rapidly changing working relations with attendant insecurity. In this context, education and training become vehicles for "self-awareness, belonging, advancement, and self-fulfilment", and the key to empowering the individual. The society of the future will be a *learning society*, and the *learning relationship* will become its dominant structural feature. The European Union's future will depend upon its ability to manage the achievement of this *learning society.*

The commission's White Paper, launched at the end of 1995, by the European Commissioner, Madame Edith Cresson, has two parts: an analysis and a statement of objectives. (European Union, 1995). First, it examines the impact of the information revolution, internationalisation, and the accelerating growth of scientific and technological knowledge.

Information technology has changed the nature of work and the organisation of production. Mass production has declined and is being replaced by *customised* production, full-time permanent work is on the decline, and corporations are becoming decentralised, sub-contracting and requiring more flexibility. The content of work is increasingly made up of intelligent tasks requiring initiative and the ability to adapt. Internationalisation is creating a global labour market, with a free movement of capital goods and services. Europe needs to improve its economic competitiveness. Developments in scientific and technological knowledge mean that industry relies increasingly on science to develop new products but, at the same time, science is seen as a threat to the environment and a challenge to traditional morals.

Exclusion. The consequence is a growing rift between those who can interpret the forces at work, those who can only use them, and those who are pushed out of mainstream society and have to rely upon welfare. To counteract these tendencies, CRET believes it essential to provide a broad knowledge base and critical education for all people throughout their lives so that they can develop their potential. A person must not simply be seen as "a tool at the service of the economy" (p.9). The future of European culture depends on its capacity to equip young people to think critically: a curriculum that includes scientific awareness, literature, and philosophy is necessary if European society is to be open, multicultural, and democratic. In addition, individuals, to assist their employment, need to acquire transferable technical knowledge resting on a broad basic foundation as well as proficiency in at least two foreign languages.

CRET objectives. The aim of CRET is to assist in building the European *learning society* by pursuing five general objectives. The first is the encouragement of new knowledge to be achieved by the provision of a multitude of incentives, including the identification of key skills and the best ways of acquiring, assessing, and certifying them, and the development of multimedia educational software.   The second involves bringing schools and the business sector closer together by opening up education to the world of work, involving companies in training, and the promotion of training schemes. A third objective is to combat social and economic exclusion, or marginalisation, by, for example, back-to-work schemes, *second chance* schools, and schemes of voluntary service.   Fourthly, CRET is determined to promote proficiency in three community languages, as languages are the key to European understanding, expand cultural horizons and, when learned from an early age, contribute to success at school.

The fifth objective is to treat capital investment and investment in training on an equal basis, or, in other words, to consider investment in labour through the provision of skill training as a company asset to be entered on the balance sheet as part of a firm's intangible assets.   There is a clear commitment to promoting investment in human resources.

The European White Paper on education and training provides a far broader justificatory scheme for further education than that underlying the British government's policy of the last fifteen years.   In particular, it recognises the role of education in support of citizenship, culture, and self development, and reconceptualises the social mobility/equality of opportunity aims described above in terms of *empowerment* and measures to combat *exclusion* or marginalisation.   Put more positively, CRET emphasises the important part further education has to play in community integration - a new and distinctive aim.

Chapter Four

Users of the further education curriculum
- for whom?

From the 19th century, further education institutions have provided courses serving the needs of a complex industrial society differentiated in terms of social class, age, gender roles, and, latterly, race. Colleges have been made use of by a range of social groups for a variety of purposes, but especially for the acquisition of occupational skills - thus meeting both individual and employer aspirations. This chapter examines further education users by broad social category, the impact of the curriculum upon them, and the way it has, or has not, been adapted to meet their needs.

Increased demand and expanded numbers

The changing social class and occupational structure has led to an increase in the demand for further education, while further education, by providing training in new techniques, has supported the emergence of different occupational groupings. Indeed, it is generally believed that the system of further education has contributed to the social mobility of individuals and groups and to changing social class and occupational structures. Historically, further education has prepared individuals, drawn in the main from middle-ranking social strata, for the steadily accelerating process of social change brought about by the application of advances in science and technology to the forces of production, distribution, and exchange. As an institution, further education is not only located within the class structure, drawing its students in the main from skilled and now increasingly semi-skilled family backgrounds, but is part of the process of altering that structure.

In general terms, further education has responded to the demand for a larger number of more highly or differently skilled workers - especially those with professional, technical, and craft expertise. In the 50 years, 1910 to 1960, the number of students in grant-aided further education establishments increased from just over 1/2 million to just over 2 million. (These figures would have included a proportion of what would now be classified as students in higher education.) Engineering and technology dominated after the Second World War but, by 1975, social, administrative, and business studies were coming to the fore.   In recent years, the requirement has been for increasing numbers of workers for the developing service and knowledge industries - which require higher levels of literacy, numeracy, and person skills. By 1994-95, colleges in the further education sector in England provided courses for 3.2 million people, of which 2.4 million were enrolled on FEFC-funded provision (i.e. 0.8 million students who were not FEFC funded were also enrolled at colleges) (FEFC, 1996e).

The kinds of user of further education have changed in response to social class aspirations, occupational needs, new patterns of education and training, and role expectations. Further education now provides for people from a broader range of social class background (but by no means the full range), for more adults as education becomes dissociated from childhood upbringing, for the increased numbers of women requiring work in the expanding service industries, and for students from a wider ability range as the number of unskilled jobs falls and the competition for work intensifies. In addition, since the 1950s, further education has provided opportunities for racial minority students requiring post-school education and for people with learning difficulties and disabilities.

Social-class basis

Historically, further education institutions have grown up to serve the educational and career aspirations of distinctive occupationally-defined social strata. The past and current selection of knowledge that distinguishes the further education curriculum is closely related to the functions performed by these strata. Accordingly, any study of the further education curriculum which did not mention its social-class basis would be incomplete.

As a broad generalisation, technical education coalesced around the education of young people from groups, such as lower professions, tradespeople, and skilled workers, to the exclusion of the upper and middle classes whose children stayed at school to 18 or went to university, and the semi and unskilled working class whose children began work at the earliest possible age and gained any necessary experience they needed on the job. Consequently, in institutional terms, technical education came to be situated between the elementary or junior secondary schools on the one hand, and the grammar schools (senior classes), public schools, and universities on the other.

The census of 1911 grouped occupations on the basis of their social standing into five social classes: professional, intermediate, skilled, partly-skilled, and unskilled. Working with census data, historians have tried to reconstruct the changing size and characteristics of social classes over the last 150 years. There has been a steady decline in the size of the partly-skilled and unskilled categories, as mining and agricultural sectors contracted, and an increase of intermediate and skilled occupations, attributed to the growing numbers of managers, teachers, draughtsmen, and engineers. By 1951, half the adult male population was classified as *skilled*. In 1971, the *skilled* category was divided into Class III N for skilled non-manual occupations and Class III M for skilled manual. (Lawton, R., 1978).

These changes have corresponded in rough and ready terms to the changes in the further education curriculum: the increase in skilled workers and the expansion of college provision; the increase in skilled non-manual categories and the expansion of courses for technicians and workers in business, commerce, and service industries; the decline of manual work, heavy engineering, and extractive industries, and the contraction of mining, construction, and engineering departments. Colleges are still providing largely for the education of people seeking to enter intermediate and skilled occupations and, to this purpose, recruiting school-leavers and partly-skilled adults. Far greater effort is also at last being expended on efforts to attract unskilled workers.

According to the FEFC (1996e), students in the sector (funded by the Funding Council) were studying for 3.9 million qualifications, 4 per cent GNVQ, 8 per cent NVQ, 9 per cent GCSE, 18 per cent GCE A level and a remaining 61 per cent for vocational qualifications other than GNVQ and NVQ - or nearly three quarters *vocational* qualifications.

In the drive to increase the amount and level of training and to reskill and upskill those sections of the population whose existing skills are no longer required, further education has begun to respond to the needs of the unemployed and others - such as former family carers - seeking to return work. Many colleges have large numbers of unemployed part-time students studying under the so-called 21-hour (now 16-hour) rule which enables them to continue to draw unemployment benefit, or Job Seekers' Allowance, providing they remain available for work.

In the 1980s, in a context of continuing high unemployment levels, a series of projects, sponsored by the DES and the National Institute of Adult Continuing Education (NIACE) under the title REPLAN, was aimed at improving the education and training available for the adult unemployed. Unemployed adults want jobs, money and security. Because they see education as either linked to schools and hence full of negative associations or akin to recreational evening classes and therefore largely irrelevant to their situation, it has proved difficult for colleges to relate directly to their needs (Johnston, 1987, p 56). NIACE advocated a model of developing an educational dialogue with unemployed people, involving first-contact strategies (network links, guidance sessions, outreach contacts), setting up support groups, making available a learning base, and then providing workshops to deal with self-identified needs. It was seen as essential to provide structured learning activities to complement informal dialogue (Johnston, 1987).

As part of the REPLAN scheme, the FEU also produced a checklist for developing college provision for the unemployed (FEU, 1989a). It included the profiling of potential learner groups, study skills courses, records of achievement, nationally-validated accreditation, accreditation of prior learning, recording of competences, and flexible learning. Provision had to be suitably located, and timetabled in an adult-friendly environment, with attention being paid to the financial implications for the learners and the experience of teaching staff. Programmes had to be relevant to the business of gaining employment or more training.

The FEFC inspectors (FEFC, 1996b, p.14) noted that there had been a marked increase in the number of courses for unemployed adults, with an extension to the portfolio of management and marketing courses in response to demand from unemployed professional people. Colleges encouraged mature students to retrain and return to employment, with *job search* and career development options being made available. Colleges still appear to be finding it difficult, however, to run courses to attract and retain unemployed white male manual workers, whose jobs are disappearing rapidly as knowledge and service sectors grow at the expense of manufacturing.

Age

Terms such as *further education* and *adult continuing education* indicate that college provision has long been age-related. *Further* suggests education that follows on after secondary schooling and the statutory school leaving age, and *adult* is a separate category available to citizens in work or of older age. *Day continuation* involved the release of young workers to continue their general schooling at colleges. The concept of education has become closely linked in the popular mind and in statutory provision to childhood and adolescence: schooling is the preparation for adulthood, a stage prior to work. While this view has prevailed for many years, it has not gone unchallenged. In William Morris's utopia, schools for the young had disappeared, early bookishness was not encouraged, and old people were taught as well (*News from Nowhere*, 1890, reprinted 1973, pp.208-11). Over a century later, further education funding is still focused on the younger workforce to the exclusion of people of retirement age, despite a growing recognition of the concept of life-long learning.

Further education has come to be formed and framed as an age-related stage of education between school on the one hand and work on the other: as a preparation for work at the interface between institutionalised schooling and fully-fledged employment. A key factor in determining the age of its students is further education's cost and who is to bear it. Are students to be supported by their families, themselves, the state, or employers? The younger the students, the greater the possibility that their families will carry the cost of their personal maintenance, or that employers will be able to pay something less than the recognised adult or skilled rate for the job while study continues in parallel with work. Most younger students (72 per cent of 16-to-18-year olds) study full-time, but only 16 per cent of adults (FEFC, 1996e) - clearly a decision that is cost-related.

The 1991 White Paper, *Education and Training for the 21st century* (DES, DE, and WO), reflected the prevailing view of further education as a facility for young people. It concentrated almost entirely on plans to improve and develop the education and training system for 16-to-19 year olds. In nineteen chapters setting out aims, qualifications, and proposals to remove further education colleges and sixth form colleges from local authority control, only one, two pages in length, dealt with the education of adults. And yet figures for the sector in 1994-95 showed that more than three quarters of students (76 per cent) were adults, the vast majority studying part-time, with only one fifth of students (20 per cent) aged 16 to 18 (FEFC, 1996e). Curriculum development efforts have also focused on the 16-to-19-age group, to the neglect of syllabuses, materials, and qualifications suited to a wider age range.

The idea of further education as provision for the 16-to-19 year age group is pervasive and enduring. The present age for starting a further education course was established when the school leaving age was raised to 16, the same age at which employers took on their apprentices. Until recently, however, young people under 16 years of age were sent on link courses from schools to further education colleges. Most of these link courses were of a short duration (perhaps a morning or afternoon a week) and in practical or technical subjects (or subjects unavailable in school). Local education authorities who then had responsibility for schools and colleges often supported link courses initiatives which were given a final added boost by MSC TVEI 14-18 projects. Link courses began to disappear under the impact of first, the Education Reform Act and then the Further and Higher Education Act, which separated colleges from the LEAs and established 16 as the age that individual students qualified for Funding Council funding (although exceptions have since been made).

Under the local education authorities, young people attending college on a full-time basis were educated without charge until the age of 18 or 19 (as they would have been had they been studying at school) but those commencing study after that age were expected to pay their own fees. (Certain categories of adult such as the unemployed, might also qualify for discretionary fee remission.) At 18 or 19, most students complete the GCE A level university entrance examination or their City and Guilds ordinary.

The pattern of age-related 16-to-19 college attendance emerged, therefore, as a consequence of the statutory age at which pupils could leave school (16), day-release arrangements of employers for three-year City and Guilds courses, and the common age of university entry (19). The concentration of post 18/19 advanced further education courses in the polytechnics, which have since migrated to higher education, served to reinforce the construction of 16-to-19 further education. The stereotype, however, is wildly inaccurate, as the figures presented above indicate.

A number of factors has led in recent years to the increase in adult students. Students who are registered unemployed can continue to draw benefit providing they remain available for work. More older women are attending college to gain qualifications prior to re-entering the labour market. There is also a demand for training from adults who have lost jobs, are threatened with redundancy, or need to update their skills to succeed or gain promotion. Advanced qualifications and a highly skilled and flexible work force are in increasing demand as, simultaneously, industry sheds unskilled and semi-skilled manual jobs.

Colleges, however, continue to be hamstrung in providing for adults by the failure of government to support and think creatively about the expansive concept of life-long education, by anachronistic age-related practices in, for example, funding, fee structure, release from work, qualifications, syllabuses, and tables of examination results, and by the lack of support (e.g. transport, books, examination costs) for students in poverty and for child care.

One serious difficulty is the government's focus on providing vocational education to the neglect of those citizens who do not work because they are old, disabled, caring for families, or unable and unlikely to find a job. Existing schemes and programmes for students of retirement age - colleges of the *Third Age* - are threatened by a funding methodology insistent on qualification aims.

Gender

A 19th and 20th century sexual division of labour has affected both the take-up and the content of the further education curriculum. Women were less likely to take up or to be released for further education, while the curriculum content of the further education chosen by, or available to, women was closely related to occupational expectation and very different from that available to men.

The situation was complicated by a woman's social class position which partly determined whether a woman needed to work. A widely shared ideal was that a woman's place was in the home caring for family, although, in some parts of the country, a third of working-class women worked. In the 19th century, jobs in mills, mines, workshops, in domestic service and dressmaking, were all undertaken by working-class women. There was also a growth in employment opportunities for middle-class women as office workers, typists, clerks, nurses, teachers and shop assistants, but women were almost always expected to give up work when they married or started a family. While girls received elementary education, a smaller number of them than of boys went on to secondary education, and there was prejudice against women's admission to university and to the professions, such as medicine and law. Most of the working-class jobs for women did not require or qualify for off-the-job technical education and training.

The Crowther Report (Ministry of Education, 1959) graphically described the gender differentiation existing in further education as "the great inequality of the provision made for boys and girls" (p.338) and goes on to offer reasons as to why:

> The numbers of boys and girls in evening classes are not greatly different, and there are actually more girls than boys in full-time courses in the earlier years, owing largely to the number of full-time commercial courses. The big difference is in part-time day courses. About as many girls as boys enter employment every year; and the proportions starting work at 15 (roughly four-fifths) at 16 (about 15 per cent) and at 17 (about 5 per cent) are very much the same for both sexes. But only 8 per cent of the girls get day release compared with about one third of the boys; about 36 per cent of the boys get apprenticeships, but only 6 per cent of the girls. This is not, of course, the result of a deliberate decision on anybody's part that girls require, or deserve, less education than boys. It is partly an accidental consequence of the fact that the great concentration of apprenticeships and day release is in two industries, engineering and building, which are from their nature boys' industries rather than girls'. But it is mainly due to the fundamental difficulty of girls' employment.... A girl has a much shorter expectation of uninterrupted working life than a boy. It is this fact, rather than the nature of the work she does or any deliberate sex discrimination, that explains how unlikely she is to get part-time day release (Ministry of Education, 1959, pp.338-9).

In 1957-58, full-time further education courses in engineering and building were entirely a male preserve, while the majority of students on full-time courses in commerce, nursing and domestic science were female. Part-time industrial and art courses were overwhelmingly male, while part-time commercial, nursing, distributive trade, and domestic science courses were mostly or entirely female. Full and part-time GCE courses were two thirds male and one third female.

The degree to which the further education curriculum was (and still is) genderised, and a dimension of it marginalised, is clearly illustrated in a Department of Education and Science booklet on further education colleges first published in 1970 and reissued in 1976:

The department looks after what are sometimes partronisingly referred to as women's subjects. It is always rather a problem in colleges to know under what banner to place courses like hairdressing, pre-nursing, residential care and hospital cadets. Sometimes nursing and hairdressing find a home in the science department.... or even with hotel and catering; quite often they are taken under the broad and well-disposed wing of the general education department. If you have sufficient students and courses, perhaps the best solution is to group them together and call them, for want of a more euphonious title, the department of Food, Fashion and Health... (Bristow, ·1976, p.22).

By the early 1990s, the differences in general education levels between men and women had narrowed with 55 per cent of men compared with 49 per cent of women having a qualification at, or above, GCSE grades A to C or equivalent (Central Statistical Office, 1995 p.52). By 1991-2, 31 per cent of girls as compared with 28 per cent of boys left school with 1 or more GCE A levels. There has been a large increase in the last twenty years in the number of men and women in higher and further education - the largest increase being of women. Of the 2.4 million students in FEFC-funded further education in 1994-95, 53.6 per cent were women: only in the minority category of sandwich courses did men outnumber women (FEFC, 1996e).

But the expansion of educational opportunities for women has not been accompanied by the disappearance of male-dominated or female-dominated areas of employment or of the further education curriculum. The vast majority of students studying science, engineering, and construction are male, while women form the majority on nursing, child-care, and lower-level commercial courses.

Four kinds of curriculum arrangement relating to gender division have been apparent in further education: different, parallel, integrated, and dedicated courses. Initially, women studied on courses *different* from those for men, in order to prepare for distinctive female-only or mostly female work roles. This kind of traditional genderised curriculum is still discernible in the numbers of women studying nursery nursing and of men taking bricklaying.

Another possibility is that of *parallel* provision, where female students are taught the same or similar course but in a group separate from men - as in girls' and boys' grammar schools. Parallel provision of this kind is unusual in further education but may be found in sports and in certain courses for ethnic minorities.   Much further education provision, however, in areas such as the humanities, social sciences, and business and finance, is *integrated* in the sense that women and men are taught together.

Lastly, there is *dedicated* provision - courses run exclusively for one sex, usually for women, with the express purpose of helping them improve their performance relative to the opposite sex or enter an occupational area dominated by the opposite sex.   Examples are access courses for women, such as women into science, engineering, or construction, and assertiveness training for women.

Four kinds of equal opportunity policy affecting women can be found in further education.   *Gender (women's) access* policy aims at the removal of obstacles to women entering, succeeding in, and progressing from, areas or levels of the curriculum that are male-dominated.   This approach is often supported by a *gender compensation* policy manifested in the provision of benefits and facilities in those areas where women at present suffer social or biological constraints, e.g. free childcare for those expected to shoulder the main burdens of parenthood.   *Gender balance* policy aims to achieve an even gender balance on all courses, but especially those previously dominated by one sex.   *Gender impartiality* policy aims to alter the nature or span of the curriculum (particularly of the vocational curriculum) so that it becomes difficult to associate particular courses with existing traditionally gender-specific study or jobs.   The emphasis is on developing a gender-neutral environment in which free choice might be exercised.   Instead of describing a course as typing or office studies, for example, a college might advertise a programme of business computing or office technology.

The FEU (1985a) recommend various strategies for improving women's access and increasing participation.   Women should be encouraged to acquire IT skills, to take up science and engineering, and reject gender-stereotyping of work roles.   The curriculum should be learner-centred, provide short induction, *bridging,* or *taster* courses in curriculum areas traditionally perceived as male (technical drawing, car mechanics, computer technology), provide women's studies modules (locating women's experience in a broad historical, social, and political perspective), pay attention to the timing of courses for women with childcare responsibilities, and provide childcare facilities.   The Funding Council now provides limited financial support (through the funding mechanism) for childcare.

Race

Significant numbers of students now attending colleges in the major industrial conurbations were born in Britain to parents who migrated in the late 1950s to the early 1970s from the New Commonwealth to meet the labour shortages of the time. New Commonwealth immigrants were frequently employed in low-wage sectors of the economy, for example, in manufacturing and public transport and settled with their families in inner city areas, often in clusters of older housing. Many black and Asian people experienced racial discrimination in employment, housing, public places, and in contact with the agencies of law enforcement.

Struggling to make life tolerable, they sought to re-establish family networks and a sense of community and to reaffirm their own cultural and religious practices.   From the start, further education colleges, serving urban manufacturing areas, were well placed to meet the educational needs and aspirations of people from racial minority groups. In what ways, then, did the further education curriculum respond?

In the education system as a whole, four policy phases - assimilationism, multiculturalism, anti-racism, and equality of opportunity - may be identified, but not all of them have impacted on further education. *Assimilationist* policy is founded on the assumption that the sooner newcomers adapt to the British way of life, the sooner any problems associated with their arrival will disappear, but is extended by a recognition that certain limited special provision, such as language support, would assist in the assimilation process. Further education played a part in the provision of language support to racial minority adults in the form of industrial language tuition often arranged at their place of work.   Robson (1987) describes a more general project for designing and managing English language support for bilingual students in the further education curriculum.

Multi-cultural policy assumes that the education system fails to meet racial minority need by ignoring differences of culture and is derived, very obviously, from a child-centred model of education emphasising the importance of building on family values. To some extent translated into practice at primary school level, signs of a multicultural curriculum in the further education sector are not at all obvious, although it would be wrong to assume a complete neglect by colleges of multicultural initiatives.   The FEU (1985b) urged colleges to ensure that educational provision reflected the needs of multicultural society, to raise awareness of cultural and religious diversity among students, to use those cultures as a resource, and to meet special dietary requirements.

Antiracist policy is based on the belief that there is widespread racial discrimination in society and in education, that this affects racial minority performance, and that the remedy lies in the recognition of the endemic nature of that racism and the development of a practice that counteracts its effects. *FE in Black and White* (FEU, 1987, p 32) provided evidence of negative attitudes among college staff towards black students, who were seen as problems, troublemakers, of low ability, immature, unlikely to get jobs, or progress to higher level courses. The implication was that they were sometimes treated less favourably than white students. Where antiracist policy has been pursued in further education, it appears to have been manifested in procedures for dealing with the harassment of racial minority students by lecturers and students, discrimination in recruitment to colleges, and in discrimination against students on work experience. Sometimes antiracist training has been provided for staff - usually only the teaching staff. Racial discrimination in recruitment practices and employment in industry also affects further education by denying access to training opportunities for racial minorities.

Racial equality of opportunity policy assumes that measures need to be taken to extend provision and improve opportunities for racial groups unrepresented or underrepresented in further education. There is usually an acknowledgement of the existence of wider social disadvantage, as well as of specifically educational disadvantage, and attempts to remove obstacles to study by, for example, the racial monitoring of participation and performance, marketing to targeted groups, providing a counselling service and child-care facilities, and employing a multi-racial workforce. The CRE (1982) recommended that colleges monitor their own and students' performance by keeping ethnic records, develop community outreach projects and *special access programmes* to improve access, and take positive measures to recruit staff from minority ethnic groups.

While devoting little space itself to the subject, the FEFC inspectorate report, *College Responsiveness* (FEFC, 1996b, p.15), points out that most colleges commit themselves in their mission to offering students equality of opportunity which, in many colleges, has meant increasing provision for minority ethnic groups. In curriculum terms, this has led apparently to a rapid expansion of courses for students for whom English is not their first language - the inspectors reported that English was not the first language of 41 per cent of the students of one college.

With its close links with industry, however, further education as a whole has tended to reproduce the patterns of racial disadvantage and discrimination in the economy. For example, of further education students whose ethnicity was known, 10 per cent of black and Asian students as compared with 16.2 per cent of whites attended college in 1993 on part-time or block release courses from industry (extrapolated from DFE, 1995, p.31). Ten years previously, Lee and Wrench had concluded that "ethnic minorities were less successful in getting the jobs to which they aspired, particularly with regard to craft apprenticeship" (1983, p.64): this would have affected opportunities for day-release to colleges. Widespread long-term racial discrimination in recruitment to certain areas of employment, such as the construction industry, impact inevitably on the proportion of racial minority students attending day-release courses in further education.

The Conservative government, the Department of Education and Employment, and the Further Education Funding Council have shown little concern for monitoring opportunities for racial minorities in further education, and indeed what extra provision was made in colleges under Section 11 of the Local Government Act 1966 is now being phased out. Recent initiatives in franchising (sub-contracting) and partnership arrangements between colleges and community groups (particularly racial minority cultural and religious organisations) may - if the quality of provision can be maintained - point the way to an improvement in opportunities for racial- minority education.

Disability

It is estimated that there are over six million disabled adults in the United Kingdom, 14.2 per cent of the adult population, most of them living outside institutions, and 40 per cent of working age (OPCS, 1988). Two million disabled people, 1,200,000 men and 700,000 women, are part of the workforce.

Compared with able-bodied people, a smaller proportion of disabled people have higher and intermediate qualifications and a larger proportion have no qualifications at all. More than a quarter or 25 per cent of disabled men, compared with 16 per cent of able-bodied men, have no qualifications. Disabled people are represented in greater numbers in qualification categories that offer no obvious advantage on the labour market. They are more likely to be unemployed and for longer periods than able-bodied people, but, if employed, they receive less job-related training (Anderson, 1995). Further education has an important role to play in supporting and training disabled people to become independent citizens and to enter the workforce.

Urging the systematic expansion of adult education to include groups such as the handicapped, the Russell Report (HMSO, 1973) recommended that special provision be made for identified groups of disadvantaged adults, that training be given to teachers and those involved in living with the handicapped, and that the public as a whole be educated about disability. The Warnock Report (HMSO, 1978) distinguished between access to the curriculum, its content, and the context in which it was provided. Special education to meet the needs of the disabled would take the form of providing special means of accessing the curriculum (through equipment, facilities or resources), of modifying the physical environment, or of altering teaching techniques. The curriculum might have to be *special*, or modified, and attention would have to be given to the social structure and emotional climate in which education occurred.

Disability has been variously conceived and classified both as a continuum and a set of categories, whose labels have changed to meet the growing susceptibilities of disabled people, their carers, and the community. A distinction is frequently made between physical, mental and sensory disability, but an individual may have multiple disabilities that defy a simplistic approach. A more modern anti-labelling approach is to reject the absolute deep-personality concept of individual disability in favour of a relative one in which individuals are seen as constrained or disabled within an environment or context only insofar as they are unable to modify that environment - perhaps by technical aids - to achieve their goals (see Oliver, 1990). In education, this thinking is represented by the terms *individual learning difficulty* and *special need*, which place the onus on the educational institution to overcome the difficulty and meet the special need of the individual. The legal framework in which education has to operate also creates the socially-constructed distinction between young people (in the 14-to-19 age range) and adults with special needs.

Three policies stand out in the provision of further education for disabled people: individual needs assessment, the aim of independence, and the desire to integrate provision. The policy of *individual needs assessment* is closely related to the practice of *statementing* required in schools and is reinforced by the FEFC method of funding individual student programmes. HM Inspectors noted, however, that there was wide variation of practice in the pre-course assessment of students (DES, 1989, p.31). The aim for the student of achieving *independence* or autonomy forms the rationale for much of the curriculum, the most obvious alternative in the present hostile labour market to that of preparing the individual for work.

Integration refers to the insistence, where possible and practicable, that disabled people should be educated alongside the able bodied. Dean found that just over a third of colleges (responding to survey) claimed to integrate mentally handicapped students into mainstream courses (Dean, 1984, p.13), while HMI observed that course tutors were "moving very gradually towards helping students with learning difficulties to become members of mainstream courses. They feel teachers and students on mainstream courses need time to get used to groups with special needs. They are also sceptical about the value of integration into mainstream classes for those students who need a slower pace and more individual help than can be available in an ordinary class" (DES, 1989, p.28).

Until the mid 1970s, there was little or no provision made for disabled people in most further education colleges. Students accepted for courses had to be able bodied and have reached minimum educational standards, (FEU, 1981, p.9). By the 1980s, provision was growing in an ad hoc manner, with many colleges admitting only those students whom it was believed might benefit from the courses that were available.

From a survey into current further education for students with severe learning difficulties, Dean (1984) distinguished four types of course provision: link, full-time, continuing education, and outreach. *Link* courses were part-time and attended by students in the last year of special school. Link courses of this kind had a variety of aims: to assist self-care, give personal enjoyment, or to prepare and select students for entry to a full-time course. While basic skills were taught, the main concern was to prepare students for full-time college life and the development of increased social independence.

Full-time courses, usually attended by students aged 16-to-20, lasted two years and had the aim of developing self-confidence, independence, social awareness and numeracy and literacy skills. The development of individual autonomy was considered important as the students were severely limited in the academic sense and employment prospects were dim or non-existent.

Continuing education courses involved attendance at college by individuals from adult training centres (ATCs) or hospitals, while outreach courses were often provided in the ATCs or hospitals, themselves. Continuing education courses were diverse but, at their simplest, took the form of single subject classes, in for example, painting, pottery or cookery. Many were tailored to students' individual needs, with the basic core of the programmes relating to the development of self-help skills. *Outreach* courses were similar in content to continuing education with an emphasis on work (getting and keeping a job), independent living (cooking, shopping, cleaning, and budgeting), information (use of libraries and telephones), and leisure and recreation.

Most courses in further education for students with learning difficulties and disabilities have written aims which are broadly similar across the range of special needs provision. They focus on personal autonomy, transition to adulthood, integration into the community, basic education, development of practical/pre-vocational skills, and the development of social skills. There is little difference between the stated aims of full-time and part-time courses or courses for students with moderate learning difficulties and students with severe learning difficulties (DES, 1989, p.18).

In 1992, The Further and Higher Education Act gave the Funding Council responsibility for securing further education sufficient for the needs of full-time students aged between 16 and 18, and adequate for the needs of full-time students aged 19 and over and part-time students aged over 16. In undertaking its responsibilities, the FEFC is required to have regard to the requirements of students with learning difficulties and disabilities. The Act states that persons have learning difficulties if they have a significantly greater difficulty in learning than the majority of persons of their age, or they have a disability which prevents or hinders them from making use of facilities of a kind generally provided by colleges. The Funding Council is expected to secure provision for individuals at specialist colleges if facilities are inadequate in the further education sector.

In a letter of guidance to the Council (17.7.92, FEFC, 1992b), the Secretary of State for Education asked the FEFC to make sure that learning difficulties would be no bar to access to further education, emphasised the importance of assessing a student's needs and of inter-agency collaboration, and suggested that the Council obtain advice on the education of students with learning difficulties. The Council responded in 1993 by setting up a committee chaired by Professor John Tomlinson to look at further education for students with disabilities or learning difficulties (in England) (the Tomlinson Committee) and to give advice on how to make sure such students could take full part in further education.

By 1994, the committee had called for evidence, particularly from people with disabilities and learning difficulties, and set up working groups on the definition of disability, the assessment of individual needs, specialist support services, inter-agency collaboration, the way colleges plan and manage their provision in this area, the effect of funding arrangements, and the quality of individual experience. The committee also adopted a conceptual framework based upon *adult status*, to include personal autonomy and independence, productive activity and economic self-sufficiency, equal opportunities for social interaction and community participation, and the development of appropriate family roles and social relationships (FEFC, 1994a).

The Disability Discrimination Act 1995 has since placed a duty on the FEFC to require colleges, as a condition of funding, to publish *disability statements* to contain information about colleges' facilities for education for people with learning difficulties and disabilities. The information required is likely to include details about physical access, availability of specialist equipment, admissions policies, examination arrangements, and counselling and support services, and is intended to provide disabled people with advice as to a college's suitability.

As part of their funding applications, colleges can claim extra funding units for the direct costs associated with the support needs of individual students. Colleges have increased their facilities for students with learning difficulties and disabilities (including students with mental health problems), providing more courses with qualifications. The FEFC inspectors (1996b, p.15) still thought there were not enough facilities for students with profound and complex learning difficulties and that the opportunities for learning alongside other students on vocational courses - *integration* - were limited.

Criticism

There is a common underlying rationale and approach to meeting the further educational needs of the five social categories mentioned in this chapter. It is based on the concept of meeting *individual* student need and is fortified by the Further Education Funding Council's funding methodology. Students are seen as having individually-assessed needs to be funded and met severally. They are not regarded in main-stream policy and accountancy terms as having *collective* interests by virtue of their social class, age, gender, race, or disability. Yet the content of this chapter would seem to indicate, not only that individuals belonging to these social categories have needs in common and suffer similar systemic patterns of disadvantage and discrimination, but that the further education curriculum itself is fashioned, to some extent at least, to meet their collective needs. Some people believe that further education should be developed to match the requirements of the social categories mentioned above, and that its inadequacies arise from its failure to respond adequately to major user groupings. But the mismatch between group need and institutional provision is structural and profound.

Despite the fact that large numbers of students in further education are poor, unemployed, and train for crucial intermediate-skilled jobs in industry, further education is funded at a level well below that of higher education and the sixth-forms of schools. Students receive little or no financial support. Provision for unskilled and semi-skilled workers is still rudimentary, with little investment in the development of a suitable curriculum for them. This is a reflection of the social-class status of further education in the social-class and educational-institution-prestige hierarchies. Class distinctions are also reinforced by the separation of the curriculum into academic and vocational routes. The further education curriculum is conceived in terms of *social class* - of provision for intermediate and lower social strata - and funded accordingly.

The further education curriculum has been designed largely for the 16-to-19-age group, despite the fact that three quarters of students are adult. Many older adults and people not seeking employment are now excluded from a further education curriculum orientated towards industry and the reskilling of the workforce. There is evidence that the further education curriculum is *juvenescent* and unadapted to the needs of adults.

The further education curriculum also remains highly *genderised*, with far too little positive action being taken (or funded) to create a gender balance in areas such as science, technology, and construction (male), and childcare, nursing, and social care (female). Virtually no attempt has been made to eliminate the sexually discriminatory practices discouraging women from entering male-dominated work and professions, men from training for female-dominated careers, and manifest in difficulties encountered in arranging work-experience placements. While concessions have been made in the form of financial support for childcare, women remain disadvantaged in curriculum terms -

largely confined to the least expensive areas of curriculum provision, such as the humanities and social sciences.

The further education curriculum remains largely untouched by considerations of racial disadvantage, discrimination, and cultural difference.   Any special needs arising from these factors are largely ignored for funding purposes.   The resourcing and necessarily-related curriculum development of further education is *deracialised,* although possibilities present themselves for developing partnership arrangements with racial minority community groups.   The task of improving equality of educational opportunity for racial minorities should not be confused with the FEFC inspectors' concept of college responsiveness, which has more in common with the pursuit of racial harmony than with racial justice.

Finally, further education makes increasing and adequately-funded provision for students with learning difficulties and disabilities, but in a context of deteriorating employment opportunities, which have displaced the primary vocational goals of the further education curriculum in favour of the development of personal autonomy.   Autonomy is somewhat of an abstraction in a society which sees adulthood, independence, and maturity largely in terms of earning a living and paying one's way.   This function of further education has been described elsewhere as occupational therapy or *reparatory therapeutics* (Reeves, 1995).

Chapter Five

Funders and providers of the further education curriculum
- how paid for?

Since the Second World War, successive acts of parliament have changed the arrangements for the funding and provision of further education.   Three distinct phases can be identified resulting from: (1) the Education Act of 1944 (modified by the Education Act, no. 2, 1968, and the Further Education Regulations, 1975), (2) the Education Reform Act of 1988, and (3) the Further and Higher Education Act of 1992.   Each system of funding and governance has affected the form, scope, and content of the curriculum.

The Education Act of 1944: government, local authorities, and colleges

The 1944 Education Act made it a duty of local education authorities to secure adequate full-time and part-time facilities for further education and leisure-time cultural training and recreative activity for persons over compulsory school age, but the nature of the facilities was never specified.   Local authorities also had a wide range of discretionary powers which have been exercised in ways which resulted in an extremely diverse pattern of provision across the country.   For example, the kinds of courses available, the level of course fees charged to students, class sizes, the award of discretionary grants to students after compulsory school leaving age, varied from authority to authority.

Funds were allocated at three levels: those of central government, local authority, and educational institution.   The responsibility for further education lay with the local authority which provided most financial support, although a small proportion of income came directly from the Department of Education and Science, and additionally, in later years, from the Manpower Services Commission.   Fee income from students and employers was another minor source of funding.   While further education was largely maintained by the local authorities, the Treasury, the Department of Education and Science, and the Department of the Environment controlled local authority educational expenditure through the rate support grant (and cash limits), loan sanctions on capital expenditure, and by decisions on annual pay settlements and initial teacher training.

One budgetary distinction with important implications for the development of the curriculum is that made between *capital* and *revenue* expenditure. *Capital* is defined as expenditure on items, - usually relatively expensive ones, such as buildings or equipment - with a life of more than one year, while *revenue* is defined as expenditure on items - running costs, including salaries - whose benefits are used up in a year. The technical curriculum often required considerable capital investment in buildings and equipment, but government controls over capital and revenue were exercised through quite separate mechanisms, often making it difficult to piece together a capital/revenue package to deliver capital-intensive courses in colleges.

From 1966, national government established a rate support grant to meet a substantial proportion of local government expenditure and to take into account the varying local needs and resources of different geographical areas. The Rate Support Grant (RSG) for a local authority was worked out on the basis of a complex formula, part of which was related to social needs (assessed on the basis of demographic factors, such as population size, rate of growth, number of pensioners, overcrowding, and one-parent families, and of educational factors, such as the number of full-time equivalent further education students). At one point, the needs element amounted to four fifths of the RSG, but adjustments were made to prevent marked annual variations and to deal with rural and urban differences. With approximately one quarter of local authority income coming from local taxation in the form of rates (domestic and business), the RSG was the major source of local authority revenue expenditure on education, while education was by far the largest item of local authority expenditure.

Until 1992, the major source of income for a college of further education was its local education authority (LEA), but colleges also received an average of 10 per cent of their revenue from student fees. Other potential sources of income were the Manpower Services Commission, the Industrial Training Boards, and European funds. College budgets were prepared more or less participatively, in conjunction with the local authority, by estimating annually the cost of maintaining existing college provision, then making an allowance for inflation, and adding the costs of new development, within the context of the overall amount the local authority had, or was prepared to make, available.

The college budget and, therefore, the amount available to spend upon college services and the curriculum, was based primarily on the pattern of provision that had grown up incrementally and historically. It was not directly affected by student or local employer demand, although local authority officials or councillors and college governors might influence outcomes. Until the impact on further education of the Manpower Services Commission's purchasing power, colleges, as a constituent part of local authority provision, experienced a sustained period of relative stability and steady growth.

Grading of courses

Within the college two major related factors affected the distribution of expenditure to courses and the pattern of provision: (1) the national grading of courses (first introduced in 1967 by the Burnham Further Education Committee and modified in 1975 following the recommendation of the Houghton Committee) and (2) the Burnham conditions of service and salary scales for further education lecturers. The grading structure (in its later form) is summarised and simplified in table 5.1.

The grading of courses was justified as the means by which the adequacy of staffing levels, the size of the staffing establishment, the proportion of posts needed at various levels, and the remuneration of certain grades of staff might be decided. Course grading, therefore, was directly related to promotion opportunities and constituted a powerful motivation for staff to develop and teach on courses with a good rating.

The size of the college's staff and the proportion of posts at Lecturer 1, Lecturer II, Senior Lecturer, and Principal Lecturer level in a college was determined by the grading of courses. In combination with a unit total system, the grading of departments and the grouping of colleges and, therefore, the salary level of heads of department, principals and vice principals was related to categories of work. The course grading system also determined whether lecturers II who taught a significant amount of category III work (at least 50 per cent of timetables) and satisfied an efficiency requirement could transfer to the Senior Lecturer scale. On the same grounds (except for the efficiency requirement) Senior and Principal Lecturers could progress through the salary bar to higher points on their respective scales.

Table 5.1

Burnham Course Categories (1979)

Grade Category	Criteria	Examples	Hourly Part-time Lecturer Rate *
I	Taught courses or research programmes leading to a higher degree; courses leading to qualifications agreed to be of post graduate standard - with a prerequisite of a first degree or equivalent.		£7.21
II/III	Courses above Ordinary National Certificate standard and leading directly to university degrees; courses with entry standards equivalent to one or two A levels.	PGCE. Craft 5 and above (vertical extension). Technician 4 and above. TEC to HNC.	£7.21
IV	Courses above GCE O level or comparable level; courses leading to the Ordinary National Certificate.	ONC, OND, GCE A level. Craft 3 and 4. Technician 2 and 3. TEC to ONC.	£6.00
V	Courses other than those described above.	GCE O level. Craft 1 and 2. Technician 1.	£5.03

*   *In April 1979, the part-time hourly rate varied by region: the rate given here is for counties in South-East England including Greater London.*

The course's grade also determined the hourly rate of pay for part-time staff teaching on it, as well as the fee to be charged to the student or employer. The higher the level of work (that is the lower the category), the higher the level of remuneration.

The consequences for the further education curriculum were predictable. A course's status was of far more significance than the size of its take-up. The incentive was not to expand overall student numbers but to ensure a layered provision and a retention and recruitment of students at more advanced levels. Lecturers were motivated to develop and work on courses at category III and above but had little incentive to devote their energies to expanding and improving the provision of category V work.

Provision of elementary general education, for example, for immigrant workers or special needs students, remained at a rudimentary level in further education for many years: the Burnham mechanism operated in such a way that senior posts could not readily be found or allocated to take charge of and develop these kinds of curriculum.

Influence of the Manpower Services Commission

The challenge to this complacency came when the government made alternative funding available to train unskilled and unemployed workers. Government concern at rising levels of redundancy and employment in the 1970s (thought to indicate the obsolescence of many traditional skills), coupled with employer criticism of the way in which young people were prepared for working life by the schools, led to the massive expansion of the budget of the Manpower Services Commission (MSC) with its brief to reduce unemployment, increase employment, and develop skill levels.

Its Management Services Division was responsible for the Training Opportunities Scheme (TOPS) aimed at retraining adults. Under TOPS, further education college and employers were given grants to run courses in areas such as computing, commerce, engineering, and management, to skill and re-skill the unemployed and those wishing to enter or return to the labour force.

Its Special Programmes Division was devoted to dealing with the problems of unemployment rates among young people aged 16 to 18, who had left school with few or no qualifications. The Youth Opportunities Scheme (YOPS) was established in 1978 with the objective of offering a suitable place to every registered unemployed school leaver. The scheme consisted of two kinds of provision - courses normally of 13 weeks, held in skill-centres, further education colleges, and on employers' premises, and work experience in a variety of settings.

In the late 1970s and early 1980s, with the cut-back in local authority expenditure, MSC programmes became the major area of growth and change in the further education sector. With the economy in recession and falling numbers of day-release students, colleges were encouraged - and paid - to develop new facilities for unemployed young people and adults (some with low levels of general education) in the form of short courses to help them get jobs. Many colleges found it hard to adjust to the practical expectations of the *new* further education students or to the curriculum demands - and performance indicators - of the MSC.   Indeed, in regions of high unemployment, where MSC funding was most readily available, colleges experienced severe difficulty in re-deploying their staff and in providing an appropriate curriculum to meet changing user need and the conditions attached to its funding.

The Education Reform Act, 1988: local authority delegation to colleges

For further education, the Education Reform Act of 1988 is best understood in the context of the rapidly changing economic and political climate of the 1980s, characterised by business restructuring, high levels of unemployment, the increasing role played by the Department of Employment in training, and a Conservative government's determination to reduce the powers of local government.   It is widely believed that the provision in the Act for further education colleges, sandwiched between secondary and higher education sectors, arose as an aftermath of the government's decision to delegate financial power to schools and to transfer funding for polytechnics from LEAs to the new Polytechnics and Colleges Funding Council.   The Act appears to have adopted the school model for further education colleges, conceived as larger, more complex institutions than secondary schools, although, in general, further education colleges are significantly different from schools in their scale of operation, complexity of curriculum, combination of education and training objectives, the charging of fees, and mixed 16-19 and adult student populations. (By way of comparison, some four years later, the Further and Higher Education Act, in setting up the Further Education Funding Councils, applied the 1988 polytechnic funding recipe to further education.)

The Education Reform Act of 1988 left the responsibility for the strategic planning and funding of further education colleges with local authorities but changed the method of funding from the historical one described above to one based on a formula related to student numbers.   Delegated financial and staffing powers also gave colleges greater independence from the local authorities, as did the reduction of LEA members on college governing bodies, whose representation was limited to one-fifth of the total number of governors. The Act provided that at least half of governor membership should represent business, industrial, professional, and other employment interests, thus underlining the government's perception of further education as a preparation for employment.   The Act also provided a new definition of further education, excluding both higher education, and education provided for those over compulsory school age in schools (DES, 1988a).

Local authorities were required to submit for approval to the Secretary of State a scheme for delegating to their further education colleges financial and other responsibilities as part of an LEA strategic plan.   LEAs were expected to review, on an annual basis, the contribution that each college should make to the existing pattern of provision in order to ensure it met an area's changing student and employer needs.   This represented a new emphasis on planning the college curriculum to meet the needs of the local community and labour market (DES, 1988b).

The implementation of a scheme of delegation tended, however, to become less of an exercise in strategic planning and more one of sharing out a limited locally-agreed LEA further education budget between colleges.   Theoretically, the major change lay in the conversion of an historically determined college budget (last year's costs and inflation) to formula funding based on targets and weighted full-time equivalent student numbers (WFTEs).

A scheme was expected to specify in the formula the weightings to be given to programme areas (e.g. general education, art, construction, engineering), levels of work, and modes of attendance.   A unit of resource was then calculated by dividing total weighted student numbers (based on enrolments) into the local authority's further education budget allocation.

In practice, LEAs recognised the political problems attendant on a reallocation of resources between colleges on the basis of the formula alone and attempted to make their new formula work in a manner that would not unduly disturb the status quo.   Nevertheless, the formula approach placed a premium on the expansion of student numbers and constituted a potentially important tool for improving the efficiency of colleges by increasing group size and reducing unit costs.

The Education Reform Act affected the further education curriculum in other ways too. With budget delegation and virement, the power of the LEA to determine the size and nature of the college staffing establishment was removed. Governing bodies were now in a position to decide how and which staff they wished to employ, although the LEA remained the legal employer. It became possible for colleges to develop support service branches, such as child care, youth work, work experience placements, and welfare assistance, thus enabling the curriculum to be made more accessible to client groups which required these services. The college curriculum could be supported more readily by staff who were not lecturers.

The Education Reform Act had a direct effect on the relationships between further education colleges and schools. The local management of colleges and schools (with schools being given the additional option of seeking grant-maintained status) made it difficult for LEAs to pursue a policy of rationalising 16-19 provision through reorganisation of colleges, sixth-form centres, and school sixth forms along tertiary lines. Full-time and part-time education routes for 16-year-olds remained separate with the possibilities for organising joint programmes of vocational and traditional academic study restricted. Many pupils, in small uneconomical sixth forms, had a limited choice of GCE A level subjects, often unsuited to their needs. With the weakening of LEA control, attempts at the co-ordination of 16-19 provision across institutions failed in the face of autonomous schools competing with one another to expand or establish sixth forms.

The Act defined further education as education for persons over compulsory school leaving age who were not senior pupils in full-time education (i.e. who were not in school sixth forms). Thus, it was not possible to fund pupils under 16 years of age to attend college under a scheme of delegation.   Colleges which had developed work for pre- and post-16 pupils as part of *link course* arrangements with schools (sometimes as a result of Technical and Vocational Education Initiatives (TVEI)) found they were no longer in receipt of funding for pre-16 work. Post-16 work was also affected as the resources previously held by the LEA were delegated to the schools (see Reeves, 1993b).

The Further and Higher Education Act, 1992: Funding Council funding of colleges

With the Further and Higher Education Act (FHEA), 1992 (which followed the issue of the government White Paper *Education and Training for the 21st Century*), colleges of further education, tertiary, and sixth form colleges were finally removed from local authority control and became part of a nationally-funded further education sector, democratically unaccountable at local level. The Further Education Funding Council for England, established by the Act, is required to secure provision of full- and part-time education for persons over compulsory school age (16) by making funds available to around 460 colleges. The Funding Council has to make the most effective use of its resources and avoid provision leading to disproportionate expenditure.

Colleges have become corporations with constitution and powers set out in statutory instruments and articles of government. Corporations have charitable status and the power to provide further and higher education, supply goods or services, acquire and dispose of land and other property, enter into contracts, borrow, and invest. The corporation or governing body may have not more than 20 and not less than 10 members, of whom at least half must be independent, that is to say, business or TEC members, and not more than two co-opted members may be local authority members or employees. The corporation is responsible for determining a college's educational character and mission, for the effective and efficient use of resources, and for the institution's solvency and assets. The corporation must approve annual estimates of income and expenditure, appoint its senior staff, and set the *framework* for the pay and conditions of service of its other staff.

The principal is the chief executive of the college and is responsible for implementing corporation decisions, managing the institution, and giving leadership. In regard to the curriculum, the principal is expected, after consulting with the Academic Board, to determine the college's academic activities and to maintain student discipline. The Academic Board advises the principal on the standards, planning, co-ordination, development, and oversight of the academic work of the institution, including arrangements for the admission, assessment, and examination of students. (*Education (Government of Further Education Corporations) Regulations 1992*).

The Further and Higher Education Act finally brought about the legal separation of colleges from local authorities, set up the Further Education

Funding Councils to fund further education and sixth-form colleges in England and Wales, and provided a new legal definition of further education in terms of those courses of further education that the government, through the Funding Councils, was prepared to fund (Schedule 2). In terms of traditional further education, the significant exclusion from the list or schedule were "courses for the leisure interests of adults" - previously referred to as *non-vocational courses*, recently termed *non-Schedule 2* work.

The Further Education Funding Council

With responsibility for funding around 460 colleges in England, the Funding Council had to establish a mechanism to dispense its money. The government required the Council to improve college efficiency, encourage colleges to seek funding from alternative private sources, provide incentives to colleges to expand, support provision for students with learning difficulties, stabilise funding, and make funding allocations conditional on the delivery of a specified level of service. With parallels that might be drawn with the National Health Service, the Funding Council constituted, in effect, a colossal national purchaser of further education from hundreds of small college providers.

Attempting for the first time to establish a new national market for further education, the national FEFC purchaser found itself with an extremely complex task. Colleges differed in the range and level of the courses they provided: there were general colleges of further education, specialist sixth-form colleges, tertiary colleges, agricultural colleges, art colleges, and other specially designated and residential foundations. Colleges served varied populations, differentiated in terms of urban and rural catchment, and social class and racial composition. Various curriculum traditions were represented. Geographical location often determined whether colleges found themselves in competition with other institutions.

Colleges also varied immensely in the levels of historical funding they received from their supporting local authorities and in the cost of provision measured as a unit of resource (the college budget divided by the number of full-time equivalent students). The Funding Council (for England) rapidly established that the level of funding per student (unit of funding) for 460 or so colleges in 1992/93 ranged from £1,486 to £5,579.

The situation was complicated, too, by other factors such as the amount of higher education and non-scheduled 2 work, receipts of European money,

quality of accommodation, and number of a college's sites. To add to the complexity, provision for different kinds of education and training varied greatly in cost, for example, workshop or classroom, construction training or general social science teaching, as did arrangements for different client groups: for example, the 16 to 19 age group, the adult unemployed, women returners, and students with learning difficulties.

The Funding Council was faced with the task of developing a method of funding that increased the number of students in further education and achieved national training and education targets - but at lower unit costs. At the same time, it had to eradicate the wide national variations in the cost of provision, but to avoid putting out of business providers or distinctive areas of education and training (see also Reeves, 1995).

The funding methodology adopted has been modified each year but was first proposed in broad terms in *Funding Learning* (FEFC, 1992a). In briefest outline, the Funding Council distinguishes between three kinds of funding: *core, additional,* and *demand-led*. A college's *core* funding for the current year consists of 90 per cent of its previous year's gross allocation from the Council and this is meant to provide an element of budgetary stability. *Additional* or *marginal* funding (at a standard rate per unit) is based on achievement of units (related to the current year's annual student enrolments) to a target previously agreed between the Council and college. The target has to be achieved if a college's projected budget is to be maintained. The *demand-led* element (paid at a much lower rate) is an amount the council is prepared to pay the college for units it achieves in excess of its annual target agreed with the Council. The overall effects of this approach are an expansion of provision, and a convergence in costs (downwards) between colleges. Colleges, whose costs are relatively low to begin with, are forced to expand and to achieve even lower costs. The curriculum has to be delivered with less and less funding per head of student, with consequences which are spelled out in the section on efficiency below.

The Funding Council funds an individual student's *learning programme,* which is defined as "all of a student's learning activities towards their primary learning goal", which involve the use of college resources. The *primary learning goal* is "the end-point qualification...... to be achieved by the student within a minimum period of 12 months." The value of each learning programme is calculated on the basis of a tariff using a currency of funding units. Six elements of a student's learning programme are distinguished, each with its allocation of units: *entry* (for assessment, guidance, enrolment), *on-programme* (for tuition, assessment, student support activities), *achievement* (for achieving the primary learning goal), *tuition fee remission* (for the unemployed, and others in receipt of benefit), *childcare support* (for certain groups of people on low income), and *additional support,* (support over and above what is normally provided on a standard learning programme, often arising from a learning difficulty or disability, or a literacy, numeracy, or language support requirement) (FEFC, 1995a).

The council not only requires each individual learning programme to have a primary learning goal or qualification aim, but increasingly lists numbers of qualifications individually, together with the funding units accruing for on-programme, fee remission, childcare, and achievement, etc. For example, a BTEC National Diploma (2 year course) earns 168 basic on-programme units, while a single GCE A level earns 18.4.   Where programmes are not individually listed (and, for 1995-96, 65 per cent were listed), they are assigned to six load bands defined by the number of *guided learning hours* allocated to the programme per year. The value of the basic on-programme units for each load band is meant to reflect the average cost of running that programme. There is also a weighting related to the expense of running a programme in a particular subject area, e.g. in construction, engineering, art and design, business, or science. The load bands run from Band 1 (9 to 59 hours per year), with a basic on-programme unit allocation of 3.8, to Band 6 (at least 450 hours/year) with an allocation of 84 units (see table 5.2). All further education programmes require a nationally-recognised qualification aim, and in 1996-97, college certificates are no longer recognised as qualifications for funding purposes (FEFC, 1995a).

The further education curriculum is profoundly affected by this funding regime. A national market in education and training has been created, with a standard rate operating through a formula to level out historical differences in the cost of particular learning programmes. The intention is that any training provider, private or public, may apply to the Funding Council to deliver training as long as price and quality requirements are satisfied. The government, through the Funding Council, is attempting to purchase education and training at lower and lower prices from numerous competing suppliers. The resulting curriculum is intended primarily as a means of equipping the nation's future and existing labour force with the knowledge and skills necessary to compete in the global economy. It succeeds in meeting the educational needs of individuals only insofar as they correspond with this aim.

The government's purpose, supported by the method of funding, is to expand participation in further education and training at minimum cost and to raise qualification levels. Funding is based, not on a course, ciass, or group, but on the individual student and is related to a learning objective to be achieved to a time-scale. The form of payment is intended to encourage colleges to enrol increased numbers on programmes, to retain students until the completion of their studies, and to reward achievement, particularly as it contributes to the National Training and Education Targets. A premium is placed on student *progression* and *achievement*.

The special individual needs of students (and the legal requirement of the Funding Council to support special needs students) are recognised in the possibilities for making available additional funded support for students with learning difficulties and disabilities or who need extra help with language. Basic skills programmes are also well treated under the funding unit tariff. Assistance to unemployed students, those in receipt of benefit, and women returners is provided by an allocation, per individual learning programme, of funding units to pay for fee remission and child care support. No distinction in funding is made between full- and part-time modes of attendance: the amount is based on the particular learning programme or load band and its tariff rating.

The funding method is intended to reflect the estimated cost of the provision and to meet the perceived needs of certain kinds of student. Unsurprisingly, however, colleges report an increase in the number of part-time students, and in adult basic skills, special needs programmes, and additional support. Conversely, anxiety has been expressed as to whether the cost weighting factor attached to programmes in areas such as construction is sufficient to pay for the full cost of the provision and to ensure its longer-term survival.

Initially, the tariff was derived factually from the estimated real cost of provision. As the tariff weightings become familiar to college providers, there is a growing recognition of the possibilities for maximising income by the selection and modification of programmes and services. Increasingly, the tariff is applied evaluatively, becoming a driving (or causal) force in shaping the curriculum. For example, as managers become conscious that funding is unavailable for any extra time expended, they will reduce the duration of programmes exceeding the maximum 450 annual resourced hours (and those above load-band average) in the load-band weighting. All courses lacking recognised qualification aims will also be eliminated, unless alternative non-FEFC funding sources are available.

Efficiency and the further education curriculum

The pressure on colleges to become more efficient was apparent long before the Funding Council came into being. The influential publication *Managing Colleges Efficiently* (DES and WO, 1987) recommended that nationally-accepted efficiency indicators, such as the staff-student ratio (SSR) and the cost per full-time equivalent student enrolled on a course, be brought into general use in colleges within a maximum of five years and recommended a national SSR target of 11.4:1, to be achieved by 1991-92.

Many of the essential features of the developing college curriculum may be seen as cost-saving measures adapted for education from the various techniques for improving efficiency found in modern industrial processes. While the metaphor should not be laboured, aspects of the new further education curriculum are illuminated by the image of the college as a qualifications *factory*, struggling to raise productivity.

Changes to the service conditions of staff, increasing the number of weekly or annual hours they are expected to teach, and enlarging the size of teaching groups, are obvious efficiency measures. But a number of other developments need also to be listed.

Specification of product. Competence-based approaches to the curriculum provide a means of specifying the educational or training outcome or product with greater precision, with the auxiliary aim of assisting in the costing of the process. *Specialisation.* As in a factory, the former *craftsman* teacher role is refined into a number of specialist functions, for example, the role of course material or programme production is separated from those of providing advice and guidance or on-course/on-programme tuition. *Quality assurance.* Performance is measured, management information gathered, and quality systems are installed to ensure consistency in the delivery of programmes and in the treatment of individual students. *Non-conformity* is dealt with through student counselling schemes and the provision of additional support.

Self-service. Open learning, user choice, and new modes of attendance can be seen as examples of customer care or self-service (dispensing with the need for *assistance,* as has occurred in supermarkets or petrol stations). *Automation* assists this process with the greater availability and use of information technology and the development of resource-rich learning centres.

Speed of throughput.   Accreditation of prior learning (APL) and the development of short intensive courses can be seen as an attempt to speed up the throughput of students. *Output measures, economies of scale, shifting costs elsewhere.*   Within the funding methodology, the *achievement element* is a concession to payment on result or output, while the funding methodology as a whole acts as an incentive to achieve economies of scale and to shift work to locations where it can be undertaken most cheaply.

Summary

To summarise, this chapter deals with the funders and providers of further education and the effects that different methods of funding have had, or are having, on the growth and development of the further education curriculum. It also raises the question of how the power and interests of the institutions, groupings, and individuals exercising control over colleges impact upon the needs of service users and the pattern of their learning.

In conclusion, it is worth comparing tables 5.1 and 5.2 as a means of drawing out the changes to the curriculum that have taken place in the last fifteen years. Burnham created a hierarchy of *courses* existing in colleges and established a relationship between work levels and the remuneration of staff.   College funding, however, was historically allocated and not directly related to student demand.   The Funding Council allocates funding to colleges, not on the basis of the courses they offer, but to support individual students' *learning programmes.*   The funding, which must pay for the total cost of the provision, including teachers' salaries, is related to the student's learning goal (as a qualification), the programme's duration, and a number of other elements contributing to the cost of providing the programme.   Student numbers and student learning activities drive the funding process and result in a curriculum that can be imagined in terms of the check-out at a supermarket, with its basket of groceries all coming with guaranteed qualification aims and paid for with a quick-save Funding Council credit card, the odd voucher, or cash from your own pocket.

Table 5.2

Further education funding council - funding tariff values for load bands (1996-97)

| Load Band | Hours Per Year | Basic on Programme Units | On-programme Cost Weighting Factor | | | | | 100% Fee Remission | Child care Support Cost | Achievement Primary Learning Goal | | Rate Per Unit |
			A 1.0	B 1.2	C 1.4	D 1.7	E 2.0			National Targets	Other	
1	9 to 59	3.8	3.8	4.6	5.3	6.5	7.6	1.5	1.5	0.5	0.4	Additional: £16.40, DLE: £6.50.
2	60 to 119	10.0	10.0	12.0	14.0	17.0	20.0	4.0	4.0	1.2	1.0	Additional: £16.40, DLE: £6.50.
3	120 to 209	18.4	18.4	22.1	25.8	31.3	36.8	7.3	7.3	2.2	1.7	Additional: £16.40, DLE: £6.50.
4	210 to 329	30.2	30.2	36.2	42.3	51.3	60.4	12.0	12.0	3.6	2.9	Additional: £16.40, DLE: £6.50.
5	330 to 449	43.6	43.6	52.3	61.0	74.1	87.2	17.3	17.3	5.2	4.1	Additional: £16.40, DLE: £6.50.
6	at least 450	84.0	84.0	100.8	117.6	142.8	168.0	33.3	33.3	10.0	8.0	Additional: £16.40, DLE: £6.50.

Derived from FEFC (1995), *How to apply for funding 1996-97*, Coventry, FEFC.

Chapter Six

Accreditation of the further education curriculum
- *by whom?*

Setting examinations and granting awards has become central to the further education curriculum. The acquisition of awards by individual students is treated as a performance indicator for funding and quality assurance purposes. The scope of an individual college's qualifications portfolio, that is the number of subject and occupational groups covered by qualifications and the comprehensiveness of the range within each group, is an important measure of the responsiveness of colleges according to the Further Education Funding Council (FEFC, 1996a).

In autumn 1995, the FEFC listed 520 awarding bodies on their qualifications database. Although there are substantial differences between these organisations, they do also share certain features. The proliferation of awards in further education is, in part, a short term response to ensure that all courses carry an award from a national awarding body. In his annual report for 1994-5, the FEFC Chief Inspector noted that the list of qualifications approved by the Secretary of State for Education included 159 awarding bodies and over 2000 qualifications (FEFC, 1995c, p.72). And this was for vocational education alone; over 1000 access courses were eligible for FEFC funding.

Awards and qualifications

An *award* is a mark of a performance standard in a specified field. As awards are held by individuals, however, their acquisition is also a public acknowledgement that the individual has achieved a prescribed standard of performance.

At a minimum, a *qualification* is a specification of what the candidate must be able to do in order to achieve the award. The specification is a set of rules which must be complied with and which could include details of the subject matter which must be taught, the qualifications that the teachers must have, the qualifications or experience which candidates must have before they can start studying or are assessed.   Other rules may state how candidates should be assessed, the frequency of assessment, and the time within which the candidate who has registered for the qualification must be assessed as successful.

Standards may be statements of knowledge which the candidate is required to have or of behaviour which can be repeated. A statement of the required standard can be expressed in different ways.   The National Council for Vocational Qualifications (NCVQ) expresses standards as statements of competence. A competence statement is a brief statement of skills, knowledge, understanding and ability in application.   For example, a statement of competence for a receptionist would be that visitors are directed and/or escorted in accordance with organisation policy.   In the case of NCVQ standards, the competence statements are grouped into eleven occupational sectors and then sub-divided into small groups.   Each set of competences is accompanied by range statements, that is circumstances under which the behaviour must be observed.   In the case of receptionists, it would be necessary to observe competence when dealing with routine and non-routine callers and in busy and slack periods. Finally, competences are clustered into levels so that individuals progress from level one to level five.   The expression of standards as competences is a relatively recent phenomena and is associated, as Hyland points out, with "reassertion of the economic and vocational function of education ... dated from the time of the Great Debate following Callaghan's Ruskin College speech in 1976" (Hyland, 1994, p.3).

Although competence-based awards are now common, standards are still also expressed in terms of statements of knowledge, that is what a person can be shown to know. Perhaps the best known example is the GCE A level syllabus which, as Kingdon states, "is a comprehensive and clearly structured outline of content and assessment methods which can occupy up to thirty or so pages" (Kingdon, 1991, p.70). That is, thirty pages describing exactly what the candidate needs to know about history, for example, in order to meet the required standard in the assessments.

Awards also describe how performance will be assessed and the relationship between the assessment of performance and the standard. *Assessment* involves determining whether the standard has been met. Assessment techniques have evolved immensely since the Second World War as, "in the 1950s, knowledge of content and vocabulary and the ability to structure them in a reasonable essay, were frequently all that was required" (Kingdon, 1991, p.70).

Kingdon distinguishes between *board-assessed* and *centre-assessed* work (Kingdon, 1991, p.145).   Once the standard for an award has been set, awarding bodies have a further task, namely that of developing systems to assure continuous quality.   These quality systems are developments of the basic distinction between board and centre assessment.   Board assessment focuses on assuring quality   by centralised setting of examination papers which all candidates must sit and pass, supervising marking and grading or, as Kingdon calls it, pre- and post-assessment.   For those awarding bodies which rely upon decentralised systems, the focus of quality assurance is very different and is exemplified in *The Common Accord,* published by NCVQ in 1993, which was constructed by NCVQ and the big three vocational awarding bodies, BTEC, City and Guilds and RSA.   Here the concerns over quality assurance are in defining the role of the awarding body, in establishing criteria for approving organisations which deliver the award, and in designing control systems. Decentralisation of quality assurance necessarily leads to a proliferation of procedures, as both assessment and verification takes place away from the headquarters of the awarding body.

Accreditation   is the process or act by which the status of an award is recognised. This process of recognition is essential if the award is to have any meaning.   Awarding bodies achieve this through a set of key processes.   The situation as it is found in the RSA Examination Board is typical.   The Royal Society of Arts is a charity which is run by a board which is responsible for RSA schemes.   This board is advised by an Educational Policy Committee consisting of employer bodies, employees, teachers, professionals, and representatives of the Department of Employment and Education (RSA, 1994, np).   The participation of representatives of key interest groups is vital if awards are to have any meaning. It is equally important, however, to recognise the significance of tradition.   For one hundred years, the City and Guilds has been the main provider of awards in skilled male-dominated manual work and still retains that position.   Tradition is very important in maintaining the value of awards.

The award process itself has become increasingly stratified so that the different stages of award design, establishment, and confirmation are now specialisms. The changing relationships between providers of education and training and those who test the validity and reliability of the training *(quality assurance)*, and grant awards and accreditation, reflect the processes of increasing specialisation associated with Fordist models of capitalism. The CGLI, which was established in 1878, was originally a providing body but now is predominantly an examining body. Modernity has not impacted upon the awarding processes for further education.

Unlike *own brand awards* (RSA, 1995) which are designed by the awarding body, NVQ syllabi (or statements of competence) have to be agreed by an industry lead body consisting of practitioners in the field. It is only after the NCVQ has agreed and validated these statements that they will accredit awarding bodies so that the awarding body can make the NVQ award.

Why have awards at all?

Qualifications are treated as valid only if they can, or a case can be made that they can, be exchanged for employment or higher levels of education. Qualifications in fields associated with adult continuing education, some aspects of remedial and compensatory education and, even preparation for higher education, do not fulfil this criterion.

Until 1992, in three important curriculum fields of further education, there were almost no awards: remedial and compensatory education (made available for those with physical and mental disabilities), basic literacy and numeracy (including English as a second language), and adult continuing education. Students followed programmes designed for them by their teachers who were taught to design their own materials, or who bought in publications from the Basic Skills Agency. Teachers of students with physical and mental disabilities designed individual study plans which recorded student progress in minute detail.

Adult continuing education reflected the varied enthusiasms of the part-time lecturers working in this field. Use was made of by-now-redundant craft qualifications offered by awarding bodies, such as CGLI, for example, hand embroidery. There was also a demand for language qualifications, some of which were provided by schools examining boards in the form of GCSE and GCE A levels and others which were provided by bodies, such as the London Chamber of Commerce and Industry (LCCI) and RSA who had always offered languages as part of their commercial courses.

Awards frameworks

Noting that vocational qualifications were awarded by at least 300 bodies, ranging from the Business and Technology Education Council to the British

Travel Agents Training Association, the National Council for Vocational Qualifications (NCVQ) saw its job as rationalising arrangements (simplifying the many qualifications available and developing others in areas where they did not exist) in order to improve the percentage of the United Kingdom workforce holding qualifications - a lower proportion than in other major industrial countries.

Table 6.1

The national qualifications framework

Higher degree	GNVQ 5	NVQ 5
Degree	GNVQ 4	NVQ 4
GCE A/AS	Advanced GNVQ	NVQ 3
		NVQ 2
GCSE	Intermediate GNVQ	NVQ 1
	Foundation GNVQ	

The National Council for Vocational Qualifications established:

- a structure or framework for vocational qualifications.
- qualifications based on the concept of competence.
- vocational standards decided by employers.
- qualifications independent of the mode, duration, and location of learning.
- qualifications independent of the learner's age.

* a distinction between an awarding body and the accreditation of its awards by the NCVQ.

These six features have had a profound effect on the further education curriculum.

The framework distinguished five levels of qualification:

1   basic (matching a minimum job or job entry requirement),
2   standard (a significant job requirement but for jobs of a routine and predictable character),
3   advanced (competences needed for non-routine occupations requiring application in a variety of contexts and roles),
4   higher (competences for occupations with specialist or supervisory or professional requirements), and
5   professional (competences envisaged as being developed eventually for professional occupations).

The concept of level has been extended to indicate the relationship between the competence-based national vocational qualifications, academic qualifications such as GCSEs, GCE A levels, and degrees, and the General National Vocational Qualification (GNVQ). The framework can be used to plot improvements in the quantity and level of national education and training performance.

Table 6.2 below is the NCVQ's outline of awards available in post-compulsory education. Broadly, three award systems are available - general or academic education, vocational education and occupational training.   The other important point to note is that awards can be achieved only via an educational institution or in employment.

Table 6.2

NCVQ outline of awards available in post-compulsory education

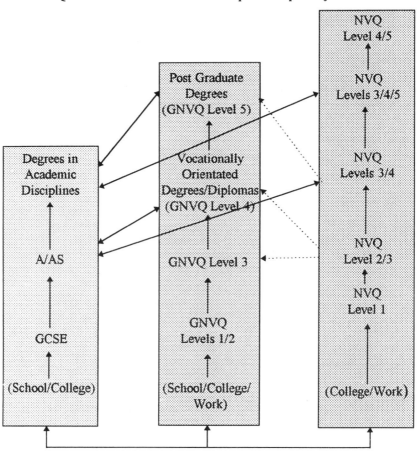

Choices for 16 year olds

Derived from NCVQ (1994), *Annual Report 1993/4*, London, NCVQ.

Awards for the first route involve full-time study in one academic discipline. For the second, vocational route, the awards involve some combination of school or college attendance and work. The third route is not yet available to schools. The structure of awards is markedly different depending upon the "choice made at 16". The diagram presented by NCVQ is not just a theoretical model but is translated into fact by the present accreditation system. Although individual units of courses taken in the vocational (GNVQ) track and occupational (NVQ) track are accredited, it is not possible to combine elements from all three tracks into one award. The NCVQ chart (table 6.2) and also a more detailed attempt by Dearing (see table 6.3) focus on attempts to compare grades within qualification bands.

A major source of criticism of these kinds of table is that the actual comparability of the awards has not been sufficiently tested.

National Vocational Qualifications

National vocational qualifications provide qualifications in the vocational and occupational education and training fields. Each qualification is made up of statements of occupational competence, themselves grouped into units with detailed performance criteria and evidence requirements.

General National Vocational Qualifications

Although NVQs were intended to address vocational education, they are restricted to occupational training and, as a result, the General National Vocational Qualifications were subsequently introduced and piloted by NCVQ in conjunction with the three main commercial awarding bodies, City & Guilds, BTEC and RSA. Wren (1995) provides a succinct explanation of the key themes encompassed in the title of the scheme. GNVQs are:

> general because the knowledge, skills and understanding within them underpin the competence required to perform in a wide range of occupational roles within each vocational area ....they're based upon national standards or uniform specifications accredited by the NCVQ. Regardless of the awarding body, the major content of each GNVQ is the same throughout England and Wales...they are vocational because the specifications are directly related to the knowledge, skills and understanding which are required for working in any job within each vocational area (Wren, 1995, pp.3-4).

In reality, in view of the recency of the establishment of NCVQ, the majority of awards available remain *own-brand* awards. Furthermore, *own-brand awards* still attract far more candidates.

Table 6.3

Levels and corresponding grades between academic and general national vocational qualifications

GCE Advanced Level   **Advanced GNVQ**

Grades for *two* A levels   Grades for *one* GNVQ

A + A or A + B or B + B		Distinction
C + C		Merit
D + D or D + E or E + E		Pass

GCSE   **Intermediate GNVQ**

Grades for *four to five* GCSEs

Any A* - C Combinations	There is no direct equivalence between grades	Distinction Merit Pass

Foundation GNVQ

Any D - G Combinations	There is no direct equivalence between grades	Distinction Merit Pass

Derived from Dearing, R. (1995) *Review of 16-19 Qualifications, Interim Report,* London, no publisher.

Table 6.4

Fees for GNVQs in 1993-4

Awarding body	Advanced	Intermediate
BTEC	£67	£53
CGLI	£65 (£29 registration fee + £4.50 per mandatory unit x8)	£47 (registration £29 + £4.50 per mandatory unit x 4)
RSA	£50.50 (£7 + £2.10 per unit x 15 + £1.50 per test x 8)	£38.20 (£7 + £2.80 per unit x 9 + £1.50 per test x4)
Registration fee includes £6 levy by NCVQ		

Based on FEU (1994) *Planning, co-ordinating and managing the GNVQ curriculum.*

However, an FEU analysis (1994, p.9) of the fee structure for GNVQs raises questions of comparability (table 6.4). The problem raised by different fee rates was identified by the FEFC Inspectorate in 1994 (1994b, p.11) when it drew attention to the different approaches adopted by the three awarding bodies. It found that 10 per cent of approvals were given where necessary staff expertise was absent or colleges lacked the resources. It also found that colleges were well aware of the different approaches of the awarding bodies and selected one because either approval was easily obtained or standards and validation were believed to be high.

Modularisation and unitisation

The most recent attempt to rationalise the further education curriculum has come from the colleges themselves, abetted by the Further Education Unit shortly before its absorption into the Further Education Development Agency. The further education sector looked at higher education institutions and saw that modularisation of the institutional curriculum allowed universities to offer more choice to students in terms of both awards and patterns of attendance.

There were clear financial advantages too, since classes from traditionally structured courses disappeared in favour of institution-wide timetabling.

Supporters of credit accumulation transfer schemes (CATS) in the further education sector have adopted systems of unitisation and there is now fairly general agreement that one credit will equal 30 hours of notional learning time, or the time taken by the average student to complete a unit. Units of 30 hours of notional learning time can be combined into modules (FEU, 1992a, and Birmingham City Council, 1995). Discussion about the content of the units has been restricted to the European-funded scheme in Wales. A debate is awaited which recognises the epistemological differences between knowledge and competence and the associated issues of the means of assessing their presence.

The only awarding bodies to be seriously participating in the debate about unitisation are those which are affiliated to the National Open College Network, whose interest in unitisation is also an interest in maintaining liberal education. It is probably for this reason that the government has not expressed any interest. The government's current view appears to be that since all post-school education is about supporting an effective private sector, the NCVQ framework is more than adequate.

Modularisation, or unitisation as it is more commonly described in further education, undoubtedly offers a number of advantages. As the universities are awarding bodies in their own right, however, they can establish a monosystemic approach to design, assessment, and accreditation, making modularisation a genuine contribution to student choice. As yet, proponents of modularisation in further education have left to one side the implications of mixing differently-validated curriculum modules within one student programme.

The awarding bodies

What are the general functions of awarding bodies? The rest of this chapter draws upon research into awarding bodies conducted by Frankel in 1995. Awarding bodies fall into one of three categories. Firstly, there are those organisations whose sole business is the furnishing of awards for the further education sector (*group one*). Secondly, there are professional bodies whose main business is the preservation of the interests of the profession as a whole and of individual members (*group two*). The third group consists of the examination boards which are attached to elite academic institutions (*group three*). The differences in the organisations of curriculum design, delivery and validation are closely related to the curriculum traditions discussed in earlier chapters. Awards for technical/vocational education are largely the business of group-one institutions.   Group-two organisations have also specialised in vocational education but are concentrated in semi-professions such as banking and accountancy.   Group-three boards concentrate heavily on offering single subjects which may be loosely grouped into one award.

Awarding bodies develop qualifications. The awarding body which owns the qualification also owns the right to determine who else may participate in some or all aspects of the awarding process. Awarding bodies in group one tend to delegate all aspects of teaching and learning (delivery), all aspects of assessment, and some aspects of validation. The awarding body will retain control of overall validation, and the accreditation or issue of certificates. In the case of the awarding bodies in groups two and three, delegation is more restricted, focusing on delivery and coursework assessment, but end assessment, which is heavily examination focused, is organised by the awarding body.

Commercial awarding bodies

Commercial awarding bodies (group one) vary immensely in size, whether measured in terms of income, number of awards offered, or number of students qualifying each year. Some have an income of less than £500,000, offer four awards, and annually qualify a few hundred students. Commercial awarding bodies offer one or more of the following types of award: national vocational qualification (NVQ), general national vocational qualification (GNVQ), and *own brand-award* (OBA).

Some of these institutions, for example, City and Guilds of London Institute and the Royal Society of Arts are very well established. They introduced awards for craft and technician workers (mostly male) in the key industrial areas, such as engineering, the extractive industries, and in commercial areas, such as book-keeping. In the last century, the awarding bodies delegated delivery of the syllabus to part-time teachers in night schools. Students took written and practical examinations at the end of their courses while results were validated by visiting examiners and through a central validation function. These awarding bodies were and still are commercial operations, that is, they are largely funded by student registration and/or examination fees. However, they were also always directed by representatives of major industries who had close links with government. It is because these awarding bodies are led by interests close to government that they have always been peculiarly responsive to government policy on the technical and craft curriculum.

Another important example of group-one organisations is the National Open College Network (NOCN), initiated twenty years ago. At that time, the only route into higher education was through GCE A levels. Further education colleges have always offered preparation for higher education but, with the expansion of the number of universities and the establishment of polytechnics, and the improvement in general education and the availability of grants, adults began to think seriously about higher education for themselves. A few further education colleges introduced *Access into Higher Education* courses for adults. A college would then persuade its local polytechnic to accept onto degree programmes those who had successfully completed these programmes. Effectively, then, polytechnics were acting as awarding bodies. As awarding bodies, they had delegated the delivery of the programmes but played a role in the design of the award and the validation of the further education college as a centre which recruited the students and delivered the programme. In the past, in regard to access courses, polytechnics acted like exclusive academic institutions, such as Oxford University or the Royal College of Music, and separate group-three types of examination board were established.

Instead, customers (students), clients (polytechnics) and product providers (colleges) were forced into a market-led group-one model. The NOCN is governed by representatives from both higher and further education. The core of its work is still *Access into Higher Education* awards. The NOCN is funded through student registration and government funding via colleges. This is the most federalised of all awarding bodies and the delegation of award design is considerable. In other respects, however, the NOCN and its federated members act as other group one awarding bodies.

Group-one awarding bodies have had to grapple with how to assess performance in applied studies. Examination by observation of practice, rather than examination by written or oral question and answer, has always been deemed essential. Examination of practice requires the teacher assessor to observe the work of the student and make a judgement about its quality. Unlike those who rely upon written examination who can refer to written scripts, however, the examining board does not have easy access to the specimen practical work of candidates.

Numerous attempts have been made by commercial awarding bodies to deal with this problem in a cost-effective and social scientifically-sound manner. The current solution is to decentralise within rigorous controls. Assessment centres all over the country are identified and approved. All colleges act as assessment centres for the awarding bodies. Almost all technical and commercial education and occupational training is now delivered, assessed, and verified through these centres. Awarding bodies have had to increase the level of resources for these centres through the direct training of assessors and verifiers and the publication of assessment guidance. Assessors and verifiers are now, themselves, required to hold particular awards.

In addition, the role of the awarding bodies in groups one and two has been altered with the establishment of the National Council for Vocational Qualifications, following the 1986 Review of Vocational Qualifications in England and Wales. This quasi-autonomous non-governmental organisation (QUANGO) then went on to appoint *Lead Industry Bodies* to develop specific competences for their own industry in conjunction with awarding bodies (in practice, commercial bodies serving further education).

Professional associations as awarding bodies

Part of the business of professional associations may involve establishing pre-entry standards. They may also participate in delivery, assessment, and granting of awards at the pre-entry stage. Professional bodies are more concerned, though, with preserving their right to control entry and the subsequent governance of the conduct of their members. Again, the size of these professional organisations and the scope of their activity in the pre-entry fields vary immensely. Many further education colleges offer a pre-entry curriculum with the associated awards granted by professional bodies.

An extremely powerful sub-section of group two are the *universities*. Unlike professional bodies, with the exception of Cambridge and Oxford, universities have divested themselves of work associated with setting pre-entry standards: this work is carried out by group-three awarding bodies. Universities are self-validating bodies concerned with setting and regulating internal standards of subject performance. Although universities continue to set standards of conduct for university members, this is now a minor and declining function. Like other professional organisations, many universities, particularly the new ones, depend very heavily on student fees, but many older foundations have large private investment as well.

A number of further education colleges offer university validated awards. Most of the universities with which the colleges are in partnership come from the new university (polytechnic) sector. Universities sub-contract with the colleges so that colleges can offer awards locally. Many franchised awards are in further education teacher certificates, providing a natural progression route for people wishing to qualify in this field. A substantial number of colleges also offers courses leading to certificates and diplomas which are validated, not by universities, but by commercial awarding bodies. Further education colleges have always offered these awards and they constitute the higher- level awards in the vocational fields in which colleges specialise.

Initially, most group-two organisations relied on apprenticeships and examinations and, indeed, a number still use the old time-serving system for part of the qualification. Some, such as architects, now rely exclusively upon the general education award system operated by the universities to the extent that the professional body recognises the vocational award made by the university. Other professional bodies require intending members to be apprenticed in a practice firm and only recognise as professionals those who hold the award made by their organisation, e.g. chartered accountants. These organisations, however, do delegate delivery of courses, and colleges, both public and private, offer these.

Academic institution awarding bodies

Academic institution awarding bodies are usually long-established businesses with substantial activity, both in this country and overseas, for example, the University of Cambridge Local Examinations Syndicate and the University of Oxford Delegacy of Local Examinations. As with group one awarding bodies, their imperial connections are still discernible today with examiners sent all over the world. The examination boards are always named after the parent organisation and derive much of their status and power from that relationship. Holders of advanced awards granted by these examination boards often have the right to apply for a place of study in the parent institution.

These awarding bodies specialise in the single subject examinations making up the GCSE and GCE A level certificates. In addition, there are a number of group three bodies which specialise in single subject examinations in the performing arts, for example, the Associated Board of the Royal Schools of Music piano award.

Awarding bodies which concentrate upon accrediting academic achievement tend to be drawn from group three. These are bodies such as the London Academy of Music and Dramatic Art (LAMDA) and Associated Examining Board (AEB) who provide hosts of single-subject written-examined subject syllabi, taught and examined by subject specialists. These awarding bodies are highly centralised, relying heavily upon centrally-produced and published syllabi and examination papers. Validation of individual performance rests upon moderation, that is the judgement of a group of professionals. In practice, this means considerable emphasis is placed upon cross-marking, that is the marking and grading of work by two or more academics independently. Where academics cannot agree, then judgement is sought from a more senior academic. The validation process of group-three awarding bodies is essentially one of establishing consensus within an organisational hierarchy.

Change to these awards occurs very slowly. This is because large sections of the academic community are self-regulating oligarchies with considerable private resources available to them. They need to recruit only a limited number of new members. Nevertheless, change has occurred and will continue to do so. At the national level, the new universities (former polytechnics) have introduced new academic disciplines and also new ways of designing awards and measuring achievement.

Summary

All further education courses now carry a qualification and, as a result, there is a growing demand for a group of educators expert in all branches of awards. Colleges always have examinations offices and some have now extended their function by introducing accreditation offices charged with the expert task of selection of appropriate awarding bodies, and of obtaining and retaining centre and/or course registrations. It is not uncommon to find specially-designated NVQ or GNVQ co-ordinators responsible for the accurate interpretation of these syllabuses. These tasks are vital since the loss of a registration can have disastorous financial effects. The change which has been experienced in the last hundred years is not simply in the scale of awards but also in their scope and variation.

Chapter Seven

Duration, timing, and modes of attendance
- *when?*

Time is one of the most important factors affecting the further education curriculum.   It is a truism that time is money but in all services, of which education is one, this truism is a reality.   This chapter is devoted to a discussion of six time cycles: the awards cycle, the student cycle, the industrial cycle, the teacher cycle, the funding cycle, and the benefits cycle.

The awards cycle

The *academic* cycle has played a crucial part in shaping the further education cycle. The academic year begins in October and ends in June and is segmented by two breaks, one at Christmas and the other at Easter.   Both of these breaks indicate the power of the Christian calendar, itself well established before the academic year was introduced into this country in about the twelfth century. It might be thought curious that the academic year is so powerful, given that many further education students do not proceed to university. University undergraduate examination became fixed in June and there they have remained to this day.   Some modification has occurred as a result of the impact of the semester cycle, apparently imported from the United States.   A number of new universities have now abandoned the three-term system in favour of a two-term (semester) system and have examinations in February and July, that is, at the end of each semester.

Colleges still recruit students to full-time courses in September and many awarding bodies still conduct examinations and moderation in the period from May to August.   Thus, although the year has lengthened, it is still anchored to the autumn and summer.   The curriculum consequences are enormous.   Full-time courses in further education frequently last for 36 weeks, distributed between autumn, spring, and summer terms, the summer typically shorter and disrupted by examinations.   Once a year, colleges are still engaged in the process of inducting large numbers of students, all at the same time. Most colleges organise some form of college-wide induction for students, in September or October. The focus of the curriculum work at this time is on advice and guidance, study skills, and individual tutorials. (For more on what *full-time* means and the length of the year, see funding cycle and teacher contracts below.) The awards cycle has become even more complex, particularly with the introduction of NVQs which can be examined at any time of the year.

The student cycle

The student cycle is influenced by the public or bank holiday cycle, itself a curious mix of the celebration of religious and political events. This means not just that students do not attend college on public holidays, but do not expect to attend college on the days adjacent to public holidays. Even if classes are scheduled, students are less likely to attend. As a consequence, it is customary to organise individual study sessions, tutorials, library assignments, and the like, on dates approaching or following public holidays.

In addition, students are influenced in their decisions as to when to start and finish a programme of study by the school day, week, and year. The school day is very short and schools are not funded to provide youth activities outside of these hours. In fact, school premises patently are not managed for children since the buildings are usually shut and, on the occasions when they are open, access to them is regimented. Large numbers of students, particularly women, either have to, or believe that they have to, ferry children to and from school and to be at home when their children are at home. Consequently, many such women will attend college only between 9.30 am. and 2.30 pm. on the days when the school is open and can be persuaded only with difficulty to study in their home time. As with public holidays, when the school shuts, certain categories of further education student tend to disappear.

In response to the school schedule, colleges make a variety of curriculum arrangements. They plan the year so that assignment deadlines fall when the school is closed and students can work at home. Some colleges have even adopted school half-term holidays. Individual work and drop-in facilities are provided so that several classes with small numbers of students can be combined. Making these arrangements is complicated by the fact that each local education authority makes independent decisions about *occasional* and *Baker* days, so that it is perfectly possible to have a number of weeks disrupted by small groups of students absenting themselves for one or more days. This kind of running programme of absences means that on courses, group activity covering more than one session has to be avoided and heavy reliance is placed on providing information in a written form.

Religious requirements can be important for some students. For such students, the religious *year* is more important in shaping their priorities than employment or educational customs. Although religions differ, they do tend to have the same festivals; thus Hindus, Jews, and Christians all have a winter festival of light but this can take place at any time during November and December. The same can be said of spring festivals which all fall at roughly, but not exactly, the same time. Public holidays are not in place for these events and, even if they were, it would still not be possible to plan adequately. These problems are compounded by the impact of the lunar year, so that the dates of many religious events, such as Easter, vary, like high tides, from year to year.

Students are also affected by the *weekly* cycle. The day of rest varies between religions. For most Christians it is Sunday, but for some, and for Jews, it is from Friday night to Saturday night. Students will obviously not attend college at such times.   In addition, there is the secular weekend which remains powerful. For people with children it is critical because of school and work closure.

While it is true that the *daily* religious cycle is largely irrelevant for most people, for some it is still powerful. Devout Muslims and Jews will not be available to study during prayer times. They may not be willing to study with people of a different gender.   As a result, a number of courses will be run in parallel: even core subjects such as mathematics and English have to be made available to both genders separately.

The industrial cycle

For most people in employment, it is the industrial cycle which governs their lives. Because of the high cost of investment in capital equipment, many manufacturers aim to keep operating continuously. Although some companies in the North West and the Midlands do still shut down for trades week, some continue production throughout the year.

Shift work is commonplace, with people working at night, sometimes for long periods of time. This pattern is just as prevalent in service areas. Here, the need to be in constant operation is less to do with the high cost of capital investment and more to do with the need to attract as many personal customers as possible. Shops and petrol stations now expect to be open everyday from early in the morning until late at night. Again, shiftwork is the norm. In the public sector, hospitals have always had to operate a 24 hour clock and it was only a matter of time before private nurseries began to extend their services.

The industrial cycle has affected further education provision in a number of ways. Part-time evening classes, so typical of further education colleges, were a direct response to the fact that most people of school leaving age, who wished to study, had to earn their living and were in full-time work during the day. From 1855, evening schools qualified for grants if their pupils passed examination in the three Rs: initially they were seen as a way of providing elementary education to older people whose schooling had been neglected. The only available time for study, whether for vocational or recreational purposes, was in the evenings. Until the 1950s, teachers in technical colleges often worked full-time in industry during the day and as part-time college lecturers in vocational subjects in the evening, thus bringing industrial experience to the curriculum in a very direct way.

Three other modes of attendance, day-release, block, and sandwich, arise directly from the need to train (usually young) people working full-time. The first two involve sending employees for a day per week or for a full-time period of several weeks from work to college, while the third is a planned sequence of periods of study and work experience. Employers were also keen to bring college provision into line with the number of weeks in the year on which their trainees were available for college attendance. Recently, the growth in the numbers of unemployed people attending college has removed some of the pressure exerted by the industrial cycle.

In general, colleges have not responded well to the industrial year. The TECs continue to point out that private training agencies are more responsive than colleges to employers' needs. Large numbers of colleges fail to remain open during the summer and at weekends. The availability of open and flexible learning courses is restricted. In addition, colleges do not in general have a strategic approach toward the upskilling and education of the workforce in work. Most further education colleges still see their primary purpose as the provision of education for the individual.

The teacher cycle

Teachers are also affected by the religious and school years but the most significant factor is the teacher contract.   Until 1994, there was a standard contract governing the conditions of service of all further education lecturers. This contract varied according to the grade but was nearly the same throughout the country.   Now, although the Colleges' Employers' Forum has advocated a standard contract, many college corporations have negotiated separately with their trade unions.

The new CEF standard contract specifies a 37 hour working week and thirty-five days holiday.   The previous contract which, with minor modifications had been in place since the 1970s, required lecturers to be on the premises for 30 hours, and to teach 10 sessions per week of not usually more than 3 hours duration.   These sessions could include up to 2 evening sessions per week.   If lecturers worked at any other time, they were paid overtime.   Lecturers were entitled to 14 weeks' holiday, seven of which had to be taken between June and September.   The most junior lecturers were expected to teach up to 21 hours per week, but these teaching hours declined with each level in the career hierarchy, so that principal lecturers were expected to teach only 12 hours per week.

Chapter Eight looks in more detail at what teaching means in further education.   It should be noted in this context that a great deal of teaching and learning in further education takes place in different places and, at different times, from those of the past.   For example, teaching includes visiting and assessing students on placement with an employer.   Obviously, these visits have to take place at a time when the student is in attendance at the workplace and this could include evenings and/or weekends.   Teaching also includes educational guidance and, again, this takes place in a variety of locations. Lecturers visit schools and workplaces in order to advise prospective students of what is available and to enable them to make informed choices.   These activities may occur in the day time, Monday to Friday, but they are also just as likely to occur in the evenings or at weekends.   Notwithstanding the increase in the number of contact or teaching hours and the lengthening of the college year, a recent study revealed that only a few colleges were offering a weekend programme (FEFC, 1996b, p.20).

The funding cycle

FEFC funding

Since 1992, when colleges were incorporated, the bulk of their funding has come from the Further Education Funding Council which introduced a new funding methodology in time for the academic year, 1994/95.   All previous funding had been of student enrolments.   Funding was not related to student (and college) performance in the way that the new system operates.   An early step which the Council took was to change the *funding* year so that it started on 1 August rather than 1 September.

But the real change is that colleges are funded according to how much education they provide for each student (see Chapter Five). Colleges obtain varying numbers of units depending upon the educational provision made for each student.   Colleges are also paid to provide certain types of education, in particular, colleges must give advice and guidance at the point of enrolment and make available a range of learning activities during the student's programme. Programmes in technical areas, costing more to deliver, are weighted more heavily.   Colleges are audited so there must be documentary evidence to prove that all these activities have occurred.

The FEFC committed itself to maintain access and, to this end, some types of students attract extra units irrespective of the programme upon which they study: students with disabilities and learning difficulties, students on basic literacy and numeracy programmes, students on vocational and academic programmes requiring help with maths and English, students requiring childcare support, and those who are unemployed and on certain other benefits. This differentiation between students for funding purposes was a major change in the funding of further education and, in itself, helped to encourage the development of new courses for these groups which now come to colleges in even greater numbers.

The FEFC allocates unit targets and associated income to colleges prior to the commencement of the academic year. It checks three times per year (on what have come to be called *census dates*) on the number of units achieved by each college which must, by the date in question, be of the proportion specified by the Council.   Colleges have money clawed back if they do not achieve their target units and, conversely, can obtain some extra income for exceeding their targets. Allocating the major proportion of funding before the beginning of the funding year, but making some of it dependent on targets achieved throughout the year ensures that colleges plan, and that systematic performance over the full-year is encouraged.   A college which under-performs at the November census can mount a programme of courses and enrol new students in January, to meet its target for February.

The introduction of semesters appears to be encouraged by the funding cycle. (The influence of higher education on those colleges having a substantial higher education portfolio may have been another major factor in bringing about semesterisation in further education colleges.)   As Lau-Walker observes (1995, pp.21-3), the introduction of semesters enabled his college to have a January intake resulting in an increase in the number of students enrolled onto GNVQ. Semesterisation also allows colleges to manage the perennial problem of student attendance because, the more weeks for which a particular unit is timetabled, the greater the likelihood that the student will attend for at least part of that unit, make contact with the tutor, and be able to submit work.

The Further Education Unit suggested in 1994 that GNVQ vocational (mandatory and optional) units be timetabled for ten weeks (FEU, 1994, p.20). The amount of time allocated to each unit need be no different, for, in the semestered GNVQ, three units would be delivered in each semester whereas, in the term model suggested by the FEU, two units would be delivered in each of three terms.   Both models assume that the GNVQ Advanced is a two year course.

As the FEU observes, "despite the absence of restrictions on the number of resourced hours which can be dedicated to a GNVQ programme, colleges have to allocate resources and teaching time to GNVQ programmes. Ultimately, the amount of time will be constrained by funding issues" (FEU, 1994, p.19).   The FEU then goes to state that "between 15 to 20 study hours per week are needed for a GNVQ programme" of which 10 to 14 hours will be teaching hours (FEU, 1994, p.19). This recommendation coincides beautifully with the bottom of the highest funding band.

The FEFC inspectors found that the number of taught hours provided for GNVQ Advanced students varied immensely, ranging from 5 to 24 hours per week, but that more than 80 per cent of colleges provided 10 to 18 hours per week of teacher-supervised time, such time being comparable with time allocated to a two or three GCE A level programme, for which the funding units would be the same only if students were taking three A levels.   In contrast, the inspectors found that GNVQ Intermediate attracted between 8 and 16 hours whilst a GCSE programme of four to five subjects was typically allocated 18 to 22 hours with the funding unit allocation being identical only if students were taking 5 GCSEs (FEFC, 1994b, p.13).

A recent study (not yet available) suggests that nearly 90 per cent of colleges actively seek to recruit students who bring with them extra units. This has led to significant growth in the provision of basic skills support, that is, help with mathematics and English for students on vocational and academic programmes. Large numbers of students have been assessed as needing this support. The purpose of the funding formula is to ensure that the support is targeted at the individual student. Following from these assessments, colleges have been forced to either introduce or expand drop-in and workshop facilities. Students either attend a centre on an individual basis, at a time to suit them, or attend timetabled sessions on mathematics or English. More students requiring and/or being funded for extra help means that facilities are open for longer hours and on more sites.

European funding

Essential though the role of the FEFC funding cycle and priorities is in shaping college and ultimately the national curriculum, there are other income sources with similar curriculum-shaping functions. The most significant is the European Commission from which colleges obtain approximately £50,000,000 per year (FEFC, 1993b). The largest fund which is accessed is the European Social Fund which funds, among other things, education and training for particular categories of student, notably people with disabilities and learning difficulties, the unemployed and women, and men and women wishing to enter non-traditional fields. For those English regions which are able to bid for such funding, it can be a very important source of income. In 1993, the following colleges received over £1,000,000 each from the European Social Fund: City of Liverpool Community College, Lambeth College, Newcastle College, and Wirral Metropolitan College.

The European funding cycle differs from that operated by the FEFC and by corporations and companies. The FEFC financial year runs from 1 August to 31 July, industry conforms to the traditional financial year, from 1 April to 31 March, and the European Commission begins its financial year on 1 January. Applications for funding are submitted in the preceding autumn and must be completed within the relevant EC financial year. This means that many programmes must start before the application is granted as otherwise the trainees will not have had sufficient time to complete the programme and achieve the relevant award. This is probably the most important curriculum implication of this funding cycle.

Educational programmes must also conform to curriculum regulations, most of which are consistent with those of the FEFC (and, indeed, many awards). Students are required to have an individual training plan and timetable, to attend regularly, to be on a work placement during part of the course, and to achieve the specified qualifications. People enrolled on vocational guidance projects are expected to have an individual record showing what help was given with career and/or job planning, confidence building, and raising motivation.

The benefits cycle

The social security benefits system has a significant impact on the time structure of the further education curriculum because substantial numbers of students depend entirely, or substantially, upon one or more social security benefit.

The various benefit rule books use the terms *full-time* and *part-time* when describing courses but, unfortunately, do not share definitions of the meaning of these terms. Definitions vary according to the ages of students and the type of benefit which they are seeking. For students aged between sixteen and eighteen years of age, the words *full-time* means enrolment on a full-time programme, that is 450 guided learning hours or more per calendar year (August to July). Because guided learning hours refer only to the period when a member of staff who is directing the student's programme is present, it is assumed by both the FEFC and the Department for Education and Employment that the young person is engaged in education for longer than 450 hours per year.

Young people are not eligible for unemployment benefit nor, with a very few exceptions, for any local-authority-funded grants. Young people can obtain free scholars' passes for use on public transport from 80 per cent of local education authorities, but this is only if they can prove that they are attending for no less than 15 hours per week. The travel definition is much looser than the FEFC and Department for Education and Employment definitions, as the travel companies are not interested in what type of supervision the students receive when they are at college. Consequently, it can be projected that a full-time programme will run for a minimum of 30 weeks. Students will be present for at least 15 hours per week during that period.

The college has plenty of scope for juggling with the timetables because the students do not have to pay for each individual travel journey. The students' attendance may be influenced by other factors such as cost of eating out, child care costs, and jobs which they may hold in the unregulated sector. The college's income, however, is directly related to the number of guided learning hours allocated to the student which must be in as high a band as possible to attract unit funding, but as low in the band as possible to use resources efficiently.

Young people may enrol onto part-time programmes but for some types of qualification, the colleges must, in certain cases, reclaim part of the costs from their local TEC rather than the FEFC. The TEC payment is known as *youth credits* and is paid to support students on programmes leading to one of the qualifications listed in the NTETs.

People aged over 19 years are affected by different benefits arrangements. The numbers of such people studying in colleges are substantial. An AfC survey found that over 100,000 unemployed people were participating in college courses and that these students tended to be clustered in large urban colleges. For example, one college reported that 36 per cent of its students fell into this category (reported in Finn, 1995, np.). People on benefits are affected by two types of attendance restriction which impact upon the organisation of curriculum weekly timetables. Unemployed people who are also claiming income support or sickness benefit can continue to claim and to attend college up to 21 hours per week so long as attendance is within the FEFC definition of guided learning. In contrast, people who are eligible for unemployment benefit will shortly be able to attend for only a maximum of 16 hours per week of guided learning hours. The rules about attendance time only apply to students who are FEFC-funded. Consequently, programmes which are funded by ESF continue to fall under the 21 hour rule irrespective of the benefit status of the participants.

It is important to note that people on benefits must not attend any programmes which are described as full-time, or which are described as full-time in other contexts. For example, a college may run a part time - i.e. under 16 hours per week - GNVQ, but the Employment Service would still consider that this was a full-time course and therefore disallow benefit for any claimant who enrolled on the programme.   Despite these difficulties, colleges can still operate an infilling strategy, i.e. teaching students enrolled on different programmes in the same group, but must be sure that students themselves are clear as to which programme they are enrolled on.   Students giving the wrong reply in response to an enquiry from an Employment Service Officer will lose their benefit.

Unemployed people must also always be available to attend a job interview at any time.   They must be able to prove their availability in a way which satisfies the staff in the local Employment Service, and there are significant local variations.   This has led to some very silly situations which are cited in a report published by the National Association for Managers of Student Services in Colleges (1995, p.6).   Students on catering and performing arts programmes were required to be available for work during the day although most employment in those sectors is available at weekends and evenings.   In another case, students on an information technology course had to be available for employment on weekdays and Saturday.

The obvious curriculum solution to meeting the learning needs of students with restricted time available to them is *distance learning*.   Unfortunately, for students on a number of courses whose guided learning hours exceed 209, or the top of load band three, no further units are attracted.   Effectively, for *unlisted* qualifications offered by distance learning, the maximum number of guided learning hours for the programme which that student is likely to receive from a college is 120 hours within any one year.   Fortunately, increasing numbers of qualifications are *listed*, that is, the qualification is included on the growing list of named qualifications with specified numbers of hours.

Summary

The main conclusion to draw from this chapter is that the timing and duration of the programmes comprising the further education curriculum have little to do with educational principles or individual student preference, but are related to a number of different, unco-ordinated time cycles, based on culture and economic considerations and only distantly related to the natural cycles of sun and moon.   Further education colleges find themselves torn between the medieval academic year of university and school and the capital-intensive or consumer model of continuous working found in the industrial or service sectors.   This dilemma in choice of temporal regime not only reflects colleges' intermediate position between the institutions of school and work, but their dissociative curriculum of general, technical/vocational, and adult (including university extra-mural) elements.

The new customer-orientated vision of further education, derived from the service sector and linked to a funding mechanism intended to drive down the cost of delivery, is beginning to affect curriculum organisation, but is restrained in its impact by the awards, student, and teacher cycles mentioned above. It is likely that provision at non-traditional times, such as weekends, will be spurred on by efforts to recruit more students and by the continued reluctance of industry to train and educate the workforce in paid working time.

Chapter Eight

The forms of transaction
- *how?*

This chapter is devoted to an account of forms of transaction occurring in further education between teachers and learners. These processes have been hinted at in earlier chapters and can be analysed and classified in a number of different ways. Teachers and learners relate to one another within structures determined by, for example, teacher conditions of service, employer requirements, student residential and availability patterns, funding arrangements and other cultural practices, many having little to do with educational exchange as purely conceived. This chapter, however, will focus largely on two related but separate issues, what learners do to learn and what teachers do when working with learners. In considering learning and teaching in further education, brief reference will be made to prevailing theories of teaching and learning.

Theories of learning and teaching in further education

There is a substantial body of literature on theories of learning and teaching. Textbooks targeted at people studying for further education teaching qualifications invariably carry summaries (see for example, Russell, 1972, Curzon, 1976, Dennison & Kirk, 1990, Jarvis, 1995). A major problem with such theories is the absence of empirical evidence about the typical client groups of further education colleges and the way they go about learning. In fact, as the Association for Colleges *Manifesto* states:

> in comparison with schools and the higher education sector, further education has not been a focus for strategic or operational research. But there are important questions relating to teaching styles and the effectiveness of different modes of learning, and about the characteristics of learners and the barriers to participation and success,

which are relevant to the drive to secure more efficient delivery (AfC, May 1995, np.).

Such research as does exist is often poor, as McCollum & Calder found in their study of open and flexible learning. They point out that "the amount of literature on open learning practice in further education is less than might be expected given the increased level of activity and interest in the field, and there is a tendency either to draw on immediate personal experience and offer case studies of practice or to generalise and offer broad overviews of developments in the field; it is, therefore, either of a largely anecdotal or conjectural nature". (McCollum & Calder, 1995, p.6). This problem of anecdote and conjecture in respect of open and flexible learning is applicable to all aspects of teaching and learning in further education.

How teachers in further education really teach

Most accounts in teaching textbooks focus on what teachers *ought* to do with little, if any reference, to what they *actually* do. Heathcote et al. studied the curriculum in all sectors and their comments about curriculum decision-making and instructional strategies remain pertinent. They say of all sectors that:

> it is probably justified to claim that early decisions made about instructional strategies as they appeared in curriculum projects, were made almost entirely on pragmatic grounds and on firmly-held beliefs. Predominance was given to the adoption of teaching strategies based on the discovery or guided discovery model and few detailed justifications could be discerned from the literature as to the particular reasons for this choice (Heathcote et al, 1982, p.67).

This seems to run counter to the view presented in other literature (Gleeson, 1989, Hyland, 1994, AfC, 1994) that enormous changes have occurred in teaching and learning methods and styles as a result of the adoption of radically different theories of teaching and learning. Thus, Hyland (1994, p.69) comments with approval that commitment to experiential learning has led further education lecturers to move away from didactic teaching toward "needs analysis, action planning, student-centredness and learning by doing". Gleeson (1989, p.33) notes exactly the same changes occurring as a result of the introduction of YTS.

A more accurate picture of what further education teachers do is probably offered by the evidence collected during the study of case-loading commissioned by the Colleges' Employers' Forum (1995). During the course of the study, the authors collected information from the participating colleges on what types of work were included for consideration for case-loading. The most commonly mentioned type of delivery was regular meetings with the same group of students, for which the teacher had prepared special materials and during which assessments of students' assignments was also provided. These meetings could take place in a classroom, lecture room, or studio. The second most common type of teaching was in a workshop. The term *workshop* covered laboratory, machine shop, vocational workshop (including brick workshop and computer room) where students attended to complete work set for them in a class or to practise skills and to be given on-the-job supervision. This category also included work placements. The third type of student contact work represented in the study was individual supervision which included individual action planning, personal tutorial, subject tutorial, advice and guidance, developing the national record of achievement, and open learning, that is, using a published learning pack.

Classroom and workshop-based teaching

In 1993/4, the FEFC Inspectors (FEFC, 1995c) reported on the quality of teaching on a subject-by-subject basis. They found that science and computing teachers give students plenty of practical work, but that science teaching was largely teacher-centred in a context where "many students experience a narrow range of methods of working and are not given enough encouragement to manage their own learning" (p.32). Similarly, in hotel and catering, the practical work was better than the theoretical and core skills (p.39). Students with learning difficulties and/or disabilities also had a better deal in their practical sessions. Agriculture had effective outdoor practical sessions but "theory sessions are less effective because teaching styles and methods of study are often inappropriate" (p.34). Students with learning difficulties and/or disabilities and humanities students had insufficient opportunity to use information technology. The inspectors also commented upon the over-reliance on the written word for students with learning difficulties (p.46). In the creative arts, "there is always tension in this programme area between the primacy of artefact and performance and public examination requirements of written and theoretical work" (p.42).

Mathematics was classroom-based and teacher-centred. Business studies took place in classrooms and workshops where "students worked at their own pace on a modular programme" (p.38). In humanities, it is possible to infer that almost all teaching was classroom-based. The inspectors commented that the over-reliance on teacher-centred methods meant that "where lessons were weak it was mainly because students were not given appropriate opportunities for research, debate, and interaction with others" (p.43).

The inspectors did not always employ euphemisms in describing teaching. In construction, they said that "most practical sessions include demonstrations by staff of the techniques required, followed by close supervision of students as they put them into practice. In the better theory sessions, teachers show flair in placing topics within appropriate industrial contexts. The increasing proportion of adults now joining construction programmes are providing the well-qualified and talented construction teachers with an experienced and mature resource which they use to good effect to enhance the learning experience of younger students" (p.35). This suggests that peer teaching or even the application of the 19th century monitor system is in place. In engineering workshops, activity was good (although what made it good is not explained) and there was some use of individually-paced learning (p.36).

In the same year, the FEFC inspected 1100 GNVQ teaching and learning sessions during which they observed a variety of learning methods, including assignments, oral presentations, case studies, independent study, educational visits, group work, simulation, practical work, role play, and work experience (FEFC, 1994b, p.19), but it is clear from the information they gave that most teaching in further education is classroom-based and involves teachers devising teaching materials for the particular groups that they teach.

Roberts et al's study of business studies classroom interaction found that the main classroom routines which teachers and students use in the matter of managing learning were agenda-setting, clarifying tasks, formulating rules, defining, giving examples, giving opinions, and evaluating (1992, p.15). This social interactionist way of explaining classroom activity is at a more abstract level than the reporting provided by the inspectorate. What it does convey is a view that the actual tasks that students are set or agree with their teachers are relatively unimportant as, irrespective of the detail, the learning activity in the classroom will be largely the same throughout the course.

The organisation of workshop learning is very under researched. It seems likely that this is the location where peer-supported learning takes place. Workshops may be drop-in, or attendance may be timetabled, so that the other students may or may not be enrolled on the same course. The nature of staff supervision will vary, depending upon whether the teachers present are also responsible for setting up the work undertaken by the students. In many respects, the workshop setting is closest in kind to the work placement, with the assessment by a supervisor for the purposes of obtaining an NVQ.

Open and flexible learning

Like the word *community, open and flexible learning* has become a furniture term applying to all that is held to be desirable in contemporary education. In practice, open and flexible learning is any course which uses published and/or standardised teaching material which the student can work upon at their own pace and with the support of a tutor. Calder et al (1995, p.17) illustrate six models of open and flexible learning in vocational education, demonstrating different uses of the key components of text, video/computerised learning, live-group sessions, tutor support, mentor support, and work experience. The distinction between text and computerised material is location. The assumption is that students will have to visit an access point in a training centre to make use of computerised material. The distinction between tutor and mentor is that the tutor is a specialist trainer whereas the mentor is a workplace supervisor.

How much of this type of learning is actually going on in colleges? An evaluation of an open-learning credits pilot programme involving a number of colleges found that only some of them had open-learning units or kept learning centres open in the evening and at weekends. Pilot organisation with colleges was delayed because a number were not fully functioning during the summer (Crowley-Bainton, 1995, pp.6, 18 and 19). The FEFC estimates that "the proportion of college provision delivered through open learning is typically between 2 and 3 percent of enrolments" (FEFC, 1996b, p.19).

Computer-assisted learning

All individual-learning proposals assume that information technology will provide learning materials, but there is plenty of evidence that information technology is not used in further education teaching: "While technology has for long had a significant presence in flexible learning, its use has been limited by expense, and by the lack of stability and standardisation of the technology itself" (DfEE, SO and WO, 1995, p.42). Rosemary Gray, Principal of Walsall College of Arts and Technology, argues that if information technology really is going to enable the sharing of teaching materials, support independent student learning, and give wider access to students, then "teachers and lecturers must get a much better grip of technology such as the Internet, and the programs now being produced commercially by software houses, than they have generally done so far" (Gray, 1996, p.8).

Confirmation of Gray's assertion may be found in the survey conducted by Mansell of lecturing posts advertised in November 1995. He found that most jobs did not specify what was expected, from which he concludes that most colleges "believe the role of lecturer is still sufficiently straightforward to require no explanation". Only ten per cent of advertisements showed signs of a shift in emphasis, mentioning that applicants should have TDLB awards, assessment skills, management abilities, communications skills, teamwork strengths, and IT expertise (Mansell, 1996b, pp.22-3). Responsibility for this absence of information technology delivery does not lie entirely with colleges. As Mansell observes, the educational software houses have simply ignored the sector. He does not share Higginson's view that the sector has sufficient buying power to make an impact on this problem.

Accreditation of prior learning

Some of what passes for education is merely the cataloguing of an individual's history. This biographical approach is enshrined in the accreditation of prior experiential learning, latterly more commonly known as Accreditation of Prior Learning or APL. The process of recording an individual's previous unaccredited learning is now a central component of both occupational and vocational courses. APL can take many forms but is essentially a process whereby the individual provides evidence of previous learning. The evidence must be presented against some kind of checklist. The loosest is that which is found in the National Record of Achievement (NRA). In this case, the framework is no more than three or four general questions such as: what qualifications do you hold?, what is your employment experience?.

At the other end of the scale is the NVQ which is a set of performance statements against which the individual is assessed. There is no requirement on the student to attend a course. The only requirement is that the student provides evidence of learning. The NVQ is a complex list of performance indicators. Applicants may be able to provide written evidence of learning, but the most common means of generating evidence is for applicants to attend an assessment centre, where they are able to demonstrate their practical skills. There is then a series of knowledge-based or underpinning knowledge questions which will be asked of the applicant by the assessor, who also observes and records the results of the practical performance.

From the point of view of the teacher, the biographical approach calls for very little subject teaching but a great deal of portfolio-building with individuals. Induction of the group or the individual involves outlining the process, defining and providing examples of the kind of evidence which will be acceptable, and dealing with issues around confidentiality and access to information held by the individual's employer. If individuals do not already have skills such as the ability to index information, sequence and sort evidence, then time will have to be given to teaching them. Such teaching as there is for APL is in information processing skills. After this opening stage, the teacher then spends time applying assessment criteria to the items of evidence as they are provided by students, and assisting in the process of sequencing work, cross-referencing the items in the portfolio, and developing supplementary evidence.

Gender and ethnicity in teacher/learner transactions

As with other aspects of further education, there have been few empirical studies of teaching and learning which look at the gender and ethnic dimension of these activities. Students reported to Roberts and her team that, in their view, there was some evidence that female teachers favoured female students and vice versa. There was also a little reporting that teaching techniques differed according to gender. "However," states Roberts "most differences were attributed to the teacher's rating of individual students' strengths" (Roberts et al., 1992, p.26).

The views of students on GCE courses at a West Midlands College differed markedly according to racial group. Almost all white and Asian students thought they were treated fairly by the teachers but only 60 per cent of Afro-Caribbeans held this view. But when asked specifically if white lecturers gave more attention to white students, only 12 per cent of Afro-Caribbeans concurred. Approximately 40 per cent of Afro-Caribbean and Asian students believed that college lecturers did not expect Afro-Caribbeans to do as well on their courses as Asians and whites. But only one fifth of the Asians and one quarter of the Afro-Caribbean respondents believed they would learn more from teachers of their own ethnic group (Bilston Community College, 1986, p.14).

How further education students learn

This section does not give consideration to the application of psychological theories of learning, but rather seeks to describe how further education students actually organise their learning in the context of what is known about student social categories and subject areas, and the requirements of awarding bodies. Again, there is a chronic shortage of information about the way further education students go about learning.

Successful learners

Roberts et al. (1992) studied further education classroom interaction on a number of BTEC First business and finance courses and found that successful students manage assessment, manage learning, and manage social relationships, which, in the main, meant that students applied themselves to course assessment requirements, knew how to organise and negotiate their own learning, and could establish and maintain open channels of communication with the teacher (p.14). The students reported in interviews that learning was a matter of trying to establish a good relationship with the teacher and making use of the teacher's skill in checking on *understanding* (p.23).

Roberts also found that group work was liked as a means of learning by most students. In this context, students use one another in the same way that they use the teacher, that is to check on their understanding (p.23). Other students were also sources of information, much in the way that a book might be used.

Student preferences

There is some evidence about student preferences. Calder et al. (1995, p.25) found that students on open and flexible learning courses and students on classroom courses both shared a preference for learning from the teacher but differed, in that students on flexible learning courses preferred to work at their own pace and alone, whereas students on classroom-delivery courses preferred group work. The researchers recognise, however, that these preferences may have been learned as a result of the delivery method employed by the teacher.

Even if this were the case, it suggests that students are themselves quite flexible and can quickly learn new learning methods.

What is more interesting is the commonly-stated observation that students learn more from each other than from the teacher. There is some evidence to support this contention. A recent study of ethnicity and learning styles did not find any evidence that ethnicity played any part in selection of preferred learning method but did find that one significant preference was self-selected groups. In other words, students like to work with people that they like. Cockburn's study centres on trainees in YTS schemes, but in discussing the participation of young women in non-stereotypical choices, it is clear that friendship patterns played a part in the selection of carpentry and engineering (Cockburn, 1987, pp.134-9).

Why students drop out

Most students in further education are studying part-time and, therefore there are usually good and pressing reasons why they do not complete their programmes. A number of studies has concluded that financial pressures, childcare problems, the desire to seek work, and the acquisition of a job, are the main reasons why students fail to complete.

Summary

Teaching and learning are complex processes involving considerable intellectual activity, most of which occurs outside of the actual meetings between lecturers and students. In this chapter, the focus has been placed on the interpersonal transactions which occur, but these should be seen as only part of the teaching/ learning process.

Teaching involves research, curriculum design and testing, curriculum delivery, design and validation of assessment, application of assessment to learners and validation of the subsequent results, all of which has to be underpinned by constant review and updating. Learning is an even more difficult process requiring the often painful construction of concepts, the reorientation of the body to acquire skills, and the confrontation of established beliefs.

There is little well-researched evidence about teacher-learner transactions in further education colleges and there has been a tendency to overgeneralise from the existing data. Teaching activities encompass instructional activities, the use of media to transmit culture, and interpersonal relations with students. There is a wide range of instructional activities with the most common medium for transmissions of culture being demonstrations, paper-based text, and talk. A number of teaching environments, both on and off college premises, is used. The best teaching seems to take place in workshops. Assessment generally takes place as part of other teaching activities but there is some accreditation of prior learning: i.e. assessment-only activity. Learning activities, in the sense of participation in instructional activities, is varied. Learners rely upon the teacher and each other for reinforcement of learning.

The chapter draws attention to the lack of empirical research into the kinds of learning and teaching transactions that take place in further education. Far from there being a revolution in teaching and learning methods, what evidence there is suggests that conventional classroom and workshop-based teaching methods are still commonplace. While widely advocated, open and flexible learning methods account for a tiny proportion of college curriculum delivery. But newly emerging methods of working with students are also noted: teachers' support for the accreditation of prior learning and for portfolio-building, neither of which requires conventional subject teaching.

There is also a shortage of information about how students learn and their learning preferences. One interesting perception is that students learn a great deal from one another which, if true, might provide scope for the development of more learner self-help groups, another alternative to classroom and workshop teaching.

Chapter Nine

The outcomes of the further education curriculum
- *to what effect?*

In this penultimate chapter, we ask what might appear to be too fundamental a question to leave to this stage. What effect does the further education curriculum actually have? This question is considered in the light of the views of major users (individuals and employers), of the government, and of the colleges. An attempt is made to discover who or what decides on what is effective in further education.

In the last ten years, effectiveness has come to mean achieving specified aims. This apparently simple solution has led to the generation of sets of statements with more or less precisely measured quantities or targets attached to them. Whether this way of identifying effectiveness is the best way of assessing the value of the further education curriculum is the underlying question of this chapter.

The data problem

There is an acute data problem. A recent European-funded study of qualifications in the United Kingdom concluded that it was difficult to obtain comprehensive statistics for all aspects of vocational education and training in the United Kingdom because of the large number of awarding bodies and the existence of different routes to qualifications (Ward, 1993, p.31). As part of the Youth Cohort Study, Payne compared outcomes for those young people who had followed either the academic, vocational, or apprenticeship route to qualifications and observed that "accurate data on qualifications is notoriously hard to obtain, and in many cases we were unable to allocate qualifications to NVQ levels. These problems were particularly common in the case of certain types of vocational qualification" (Payne, 1995, p.6). Not all students attended further education colleges, but the difficulties to which authors refer are significant for those people who measure effectiveness by number and level of qualification.

The views of the government

An important way of deciding on effectiveness and who should define it is the stakeholder model. The present government places total reliance on this procedure. It identifies which sections of society should have an interest in education and training, seeks to persuade these parties to make a stake in education and training and, at the same time, tries to identify what would be of benefit to these sections. The results of this exercise have been quite fascinating as can be seen from earlier chapters. According to the government's most recent statement, *Lifetime Learning,* responsibility for improving the knowledge and skills of adults lies with individuals and employers who "together must shoulder the main responsibility. For itself, the government is concerned to ensure that society gets the benefit of increased levels of education and training generally, and in particular that unemployed people and other disadvantaged groups receive vocational training and education" (DfEE, SO and WO, 1995, pp.9-10).

An earlier and related document, *Prosperity through Skills* (Employment Department, 1993b, p.13) provides performance indicators for vocational education and training providers. They are expected to supply a broader range of work-related qualifications, more skills, more qualifications per person, more people with higher qualifications, and more enterprising attitudes. It is also important to realise that the government wants more NVQs and more GNVQs not qualifications in general, (DfEE, SO and WO, 1995, p.34). In 1995, the government made colleges into stakeholders and, therefore, treats this list of performance indicators as measures of the performances, both of individual students attending colleges, as well as of colleges themselves.

There is no doubt that more people are enrolling on further education college courses. Between August 1994 and July 1995, almost 4 million people enrolled (FEFC, 1995c, p.8). Colleges are also the main providers of NVQs to full-time students (Field, 1995, p.36) and in 1994-5, the majority of new registrations on GNVQ courses (53,000) were in colleges (FEFC, 1995c, p.55).

It is well established that, in general, the more qualifications individuals have, the greater the likelihood that they will acquire more. Participation in higher education has grown in the last thirty years to 30 per cent of the population.

Whether individuals are more enterprising is harder to assess but the growth of the unregulated economy and increasing numbers of people prepared to pay for their own education might be taken as indicators (DfEE, SO and WO, 1995, p.26).

There is some doubt whether the vision of a market place of training providers, included in which would be further education colleges, is likely to deliver the curriculum required by either employers or individual students, fee paying or otherwise.

Effectiveness and employers

It is not possible to make blanket statements about how employers assess the effectiveness of the further education curriculum. Few small employers have any direct contact with colleges or direct their employees to make use of college services. In fact, the evidence is that this sector is deeply suspicious of any education and of anything other than on-the-job training. In the case of larger employers the picture is rather different. Larger employers need to be considered on a sectoral basis. In well-established industries, such as construction, engineering, and extractive industries, large employers continue to make use of colleges. Data on utilisation, however, is skewed by the categories used to collect it. The FEFC does not distinguish new industries, such as computing and media. The differential rates of confidence in the sector continue: modern apprenticeships are largely taken up by construction and engineering, which always provided day-release for male apprentices training to skilled manual levels. Colleges are major and growing providers of training for the health and social services, both private and public (FEFC, 1996b, p.27).

Qualifications

Although the government is promoting qualifications as an outcome, there is substantial evidence that employers do not use qualifications as criteria for selecting people to basic-grade positions (see Wellington, 1987, p.32, Field, 1995, p.32). As Field points out, "in the external labour markets for un- and semi-skilled occupations, for both workers and employers, it costs more to seek to match each individual's formal qualifications with a job specification than the search yields in rewards". Unemployed people seeking semi-skilled work recognise this well, as Crowley-Bainton noted in her study of unemployed open learning students. She found that, of those who dropped out, about 26 per cent left because they got a job, the course was interfering with getting a job, or the student believed that the course would interfere with this activity (1995, p.28).

The FEFC is also aware that students leave courses for employment and will discontinue attendance, even if the employment is only part-time. They cite, presumably with approval, a students' destination category set, which allocates completers and early leavers into employment according to whether the work is full or part-time (FEFC, 1996c, p.16). In fact, colleges operating in areas with high unemployment have managed to promote the act of leaving a course early as a sign of the success of the course. While it is possible to sympathise with this tactic as a means of explaining and justifying high drop-out rates, to offer it as proof of the quality of a course is surely an indication of the failure of the education system and the prevailing negative attitude of employers towards training.

Skills increase

The second government outcome for further education is an increase in skills. But again, there is evidence that what employers want from pre-degree-level employees is particular attitudes and dispositions. And as Field points out, "occupational qualifications which are necessarily silent on social normative qualities will tend to be largely disregarded in the labour market" (Field, 1995, p.33). Furthermore, career advancement within an organisation is heavily influenced by the performance within it, not by the acquisition of additional qualifications.

With unskilled and semiskilled manual jobs disappearing rapidly, the growth of NVQs being largely at levels one and two, and with the take-up being chiefly by government agencies and departments, it is difficult not to agree with Field that "changes in the qualifications systems are probably the least effective means of dealing with skills shortages at this level" (Field, 1995, p.35) - even were there to be a shortage of labour at these levels. The low level of wages and plethora of part-time employment suggest that there is a shortage of jobs - not skills: it is a buyer's not a seller's market.

Even if the outcomes which colleges should be measured by is an increase in skills, how, Wellington asks (1987, p.26), can skills be separated from knowledge and attitudes? The exercise of skill is inextricably bound up with knowledge and attitude. In other words, if you don't want to do something, and don't know how to do something, then that something won't be done.

There is a considerable literature devoted to criticism of the separation of skills from knowledge and attitude in the further education curriculum. It is clear that the argument that it should not be has been partly won. The introduction of the GNVQ attests to the NCVQ's acceptance that skills can only be developed in the context of wider knowledge. Furthermore, no educationalist would argue against the desirability of explaining to people how to apply theory to practical outcomes or indeed to theorise from practice.

Student satisfaction

There has been a move in recent years to studies of student satisfaction, the argument being that if you find out what the customer wants and give them what they want then you will have happy customers and ones who will want to return. This emphasis on meeting customer need, however, is in direct conflict with another dimension of government strategy - achieving the national education and training targets.

The conflict is epitomised in a recent study of college responsiveness which has chapter headings such as, measures of responsiveness, assessing the needs of employers and the community, and training to meet employment needs. In contrast, a section on measures of responsiveness opens with the following statement: "The responsiveness of the sector [further education] can be judged by the degree to which it contributes to the achievement of the national targets for education and training" (FEFC, 1996b, p.6). This is one part of the quality ideology. It is, of course, precisely about education as a product, a commodity to be marketed alongside holidays, house improvement, new car and all the other semi-luxuries available to those in permanent employment today. While it is important to find out from students if they are satisfied with what they have received, as a measure of curriculum effectiveness, student satisfaction is a rather limited concept.

As the FEFC points out in their survey of college responsiveness, "most colleges use questionnaires to gauge student levels of satisfaction with their courses but the questionnaires are rarely designed to gather students' views on how relevant their courses are to their intended study or employment routes" (FEFC, 1996b, p.7). And there is evidence that students know what they want from education and that they are right. Payne found that full-time academic education gave the highest probability of reaching NVQ level 3 by age 24 irrespective of examination results achieved at age sixteen (Payne, 1995, p.11). That the rate of achieving NVQ 3 declines with the average score in no way casts into doubt the wisdom of students' choice. A young woman with an average examination score at aged 16 who followed an academic programme had a .44 chance of achieving NVQ 3 in contrast to .14 chance if she followed a vocational programme.

Colleges and effectiveness

Progression

The key reason why the FEFC is able to claim drop out/non-completion as a success is because the move from training to a job is defined as progression. As Spours points out (1991, p.76), the concept of progression is attractive because it acts as a critique of curriculum discontinuities. He suggests that progression could mean access to courses and institutions, continuity of learning, recurrence of education, maturation of intellectual work, movement between types of qualifications, movement between different levels within a qualification system, vertical and horizontal progression, credit accumulation and transfer and, of course, transition to the labour market. His list is refreshing because it actually includes some measures of individual progression which are not qualification-related, and one which relates to intellectual development.

Is this kind of progression what is being sought or provided? Frankel's survey of college prospectuses (Frankel, 1995b) suggests that the curriculum of further education colleges is not organised to facilitate progression. Few colleges operate with explicit progression models and, of those which do, there is no agreement on the number of steps required to achieve the objective or on what the objective might be. All colleges use a form of the tripartite vertical division recognised in the NCVQ framework (see table 6.1). The objective, or outcome, is not always stated and when it is, it may be limited to qualifications or some other achievement which the college itself can deliver. The number of steps varies, with some colleges collapsing NVQ levels 1 and 2, or treating HND as a step into higher education. Where students are concerned, it is hard to know whether they actually do want the sort of pick-and-mix curriculum which Spours suggests would facilitate and/or be a measure of curriculum effectiveness.

It is also clear, however, that progression has been closely linked to the promotion of individual choice and responsibility and, indeed, a virtue has been made out of the current curriculum chaos. In fact, a whole new counselling, advice, and guidance industry has sprung up - now formally recognised by the FEFC in its funding structure - precisely to deal with the multiplicity of choices open to the intending student who is now seen to require specialist advice to make a choice. In reality, the problem lies, not with the student, but with the whole system which, has ended up blaming the service users for their incompetence in making informed decisions about their educational and training requirements.

Spours's observation about the politics of progression in the 14-to-19 curriculum could be extended to cover the entire further education curriculum. The problems of duplication of certification and the narrowness of the NCVQ approach to knowledge and skill raises the question of the type of progression strategies to be utilised by college staff. Should practitioners and curriculum planners develop *personal progression* or *course progression* strategies?

In practice, a pragmatic approach has been followed at both national and college level. Individual action planning is required for certain types of programme, e.g. NVQ and GNVQ, but its value to the individual student is limited. Funding is not now really available for non-vocational education which means that students choosing an outcome for which they did not seek a qualification would have to pay full cost. Secondly, without a credit accumulation transfer scheme, colleges cannot deliver the requested curriculum. At its worst, "personal progression strategies can be seen as a way of helping individuals to find their way through the progression maze (the idea of overcoming confusion of provision) as opposed to changing the curriculum and accreditation structures which contribute to stratification" (Spours, 1991, p.83).

Better education as an outcome

Even if the government's goals seem limited, surely everyone must want people who pass through further education colleges to be better educated than they were at the outset? In considering better education, its impact on both economic, political, and cultural life, and on the individual's life chances needs to be considered. There is no information on the relationship between rates of participation on further education and the effectiveness of that participation in political, social and cultural life, or civil society. On the other hand, it is true that quite a lot is known about the social demography of non-participants in post-compulsory education. Non-participants are more likely to be male, working class, and older, are likely to be those with the least initial education, and to be employed in manual work. People who are unemployed, or not looking for work, are also excluded, notably women with children and people with physical and/or mental disabilities (McGivney, 1990, pp.14-6). These are the same groups which are least likely to vote or to participate in voluntary work or to have access to their own transport.

It is also true that a substantial minority of participants do not complete their programmes in the average time. In fact, the lower the level of award, the more likely this will be. The Joint Council of National Vocational Awardingx Bodies provided the results of GNVQ completion within the notional time by people registering in September 1993.

Table 9.1

GNVQ completion rates of people registering in September 1993.

Level	Achieved award
Advanced	47%
Intermediate	36%
Foundation	21%

Derived from *FEFC Chief Inspector's Annual Report* (1995c), p.31.

These rates are reflected in college data collected by the FEFC inspectorate, which criticises the curriculum provided for students with learning difficulties and disabilities with the observation that "although many colleges are planning to extend their vocational programmes to such students, there has been little systematic analysis of either need or demand" (FEFC, 1995c, p.10). The inspectors also confirm other findings about the nature of the vocational curriculum, namely that "teachers were more successful in developing students' practical skills than they were in developing their understanding of underlying theory" (FEFC, 1995c, p.9).

What is more interesting is the nature of the service which the colleges do provide to those students who choose the vocational routes. Most of these students will pass through further education colleges. Young women were significantly more disadvantaged by taking options outside of full-time academic education than men (Payne, 1995, p10). Payne does not explore reasons for these disparities but a recent unpublished study by Frankel gives some insight.

The study of college prospectuses (Frankel, 1995b) showed that the classification of courses by subject was a very important organising principle but that there were markedly different ways in which this operated, depending upon the subjects concerned. Thus, while most colleges grouped information about art and design under headings such as art and design courses, programmes, or faculties, colleges frequently drew distinctions between business studies and secretarial/administration/office studies. The majority of courses offered under *business studies* up to and including NVQ level 3 were either full time and/or validated by BTEC/GNVQ, whereas those classified under *secretarial* tended to be single subjects validated by RSA and NVQ. It is also in this field that specialist qualifications appeared, notably LCCI and AMSPAR. Some colleges also offered their own certificates, grouping together NVQs, RSA single qualifications and one or more GCSEs or modules from a GNVQ. But, as Payne found, young women on mixed qualification courses did even worse in terms of progression than those on vocational programmes (Payne, 1995, p.10).

Colleges cannot claim that these outcomes are products of government policy. Cockburn in her study of YTS found exactly the same distinction was deployed by colleges in 1987, and that training agencies sent male trainees to business studies and young women to secretarial courses at college. She found no evidence that the colleges had any strategy internally for dealing with the problem (Cockburn, 1987, pp.102-6). Ten years later, the colleges are actively pursuing the same genderised curriculum.

The key question must be - are those people who pass through further education colleges better educated as a result? The answer must be a tentative yes, since people leaving further education are more likely to be confident, occupied, and qualified. But perhaps it should be recognised that achieving a qualification may not be the same thing as becoming educated, although most current concepts of education leave behind a whiff of stale high culture.

Chapter Ten

The direction of the further education curriculum
- *where to?*

In conclusion, it is worth drawing out those features of the curriculum (mentioned in earlier chapters) which, in their simultaneous operation and effects, are determining the direction of change and transforming the face of further education. Eleven interrelated factors are listed and each briefly described below.

- mass access
- equality of opportunity
- partnerships
- systems
- progression
- accreditation
- competence
- learning-centredness
- specialisation
- products and packages
- automation

Mass access

The emergence of the new further education is closely related to the gradual recognition by governments since the Second World War of the need for mass further and higher education, and the progressive implementation of measures to make provision more widely available. The pressure to educate and train the population as a whole - not merely a small proportion of it - stems from a belief that the nation's future economic prosperity and competitive position is under threat from other advanced industrial economies with better educated and more highly skilled work forces. It appears at last to have been accepted that the nation's success depends on its investment in the education of all its people - or at least those preparing for or already in employment (see pp.30-34). Far larger numbers are choosing to make use of the education system after compulsory schooling, with a significant expansion of further and higher education provision.

The process of moving from exclusive minority forms to inclusive mass forms of education is by no means complete and the implications of the change in policy have not always been clearly understood. Selective traditions, demonstrated in the stubborn adherence to GCE A levels and the three-stream approach to 16 to 19 qualifications - GCE, GNVQ and NVQ - reflect outmoded social divisions and continuing entry restrictions to higher education and employment.

Other deep-seated mental sets hinder the drive for mass further and higher education. The view persists that more students mean lower standards. Education is still generally conceived as a preparatory stage for youth, to be completed prior to full-blown adulthood. Despite the assertion that the pace of technological change is speeding up and that the workforce can no longer expect a job for life, comprehensive arrangements for life-long learning are not yet in place (DfEE, SO and WO, 1995). Nevertheless, as the needs for employment flexibility and adaptability, updated industrial skills, improved social cohesion and understanding, and a shared common European or international culture become ever more pressing, the further education sector can be expected to move steadily towards providing post-school facilities for the whole population, irrespective of age or occupational status.

One essential requirement of the new further education curriculum, therefore, is that it make provision for a greater proportion of the population. Given the present aversion of governments to increasing public expenditure and taxation, this means that greater numbers of students must be educated at a lower per capita cost. Methods must be found of organising the curriculum to create economies of scale while preserving or improving the effectiveness of delivery (see pp.65-70).

The move from minority to mass education requires colleges to take measures to attract and recruit more students, to ensure their success, and to enable them to progress to higher level courses. Any arrangements for delivering the curriculum which prevent access, restrict choice, or hinder progression, work against the imperative of achieving mass participation. The new further education has, in other words, to improve access. Colleges working to such a programme claim to offer open-access education.

Provision for larger student numbers might be assumed to demand more resources, but the task facing the new further education is to educate more students at no extra cost. Efficiency measures, then, are nearly always attendant on the implementation of open-access policies, and so the means of delivering the curriculum have to be related to cost. This is the key management consideration in the current development of further education provision.

In curriculum terms, mass education requires an overall structure that encourages participation, and a distinction to be made between selection and rejection. Those insufficiently prepared for selection to progress to more advanced courses need not be rejected but instead be given an opportunity to acquire the requisite level of preparation. A comprehensive curriculum structure is required, horizontally, in terms of the breadth of subject matter, and vertically, in terms of the facilities it offers for more advanced study. Students must be in a position to exercise the widest possible choice in accordance with their needs and to continue to develop their abilities and interests at higher levels.

Separately organised, free-standing courses, with idiosyncratic criteria of selection and independently accredited by some exclusive vocational examining board, hinder the development of comprehensive structures and often result in restrictive channelling of students who, on completion, may find themselves in an educational or occupational cul-de-sac with no readily apparent means of progression. Quite apart from reducing opportunity, older forms of exclusive curriculum organisation are costly and wasteful of human resources. The further education curriculum, therefore, is likely to become increasingly accessible and comprehensive.

Equality of opportunity

The extension of educational provision not only requires the removal of restrictions on access, transfer, and progression, but the active participation of sections of the population previously absent from, or present only in small numbers, in the further education sector. It is perfectly possible that, in the pursuit of rapid expansion policies, colleges will concentrate on easy targets at the expense of groups they find more difficult to attract and sustain in their

studies. An equality of opportunity policy is not merely another way of referring to expansion or open access but, as it relates to the curriculum, involves measures to encourage the participation of groups who are under-represented or excluded from the education process. Educational achievement, in terms of duration, content, and level of study, varies demonstrably by age, gender, social class, employment status, occupation, geographical location, ethnicity, and disability. The curriculum has a key role to play in maximising participation and inclusion (see Chapter Four).

Ostensibly, the new further education curriculum is based on a needs analysis, which is intended to relate curriculum supply to demand, although the degree to which it is student need-sensitive rather than occupationally-led or academic standards-led, remains a matter of debate. The Further Education Funding Council's view of needs analyses for strategic planning purposes seems to be based on the simplistic idea that a college's curriculum can, and should be, related directly to local economic needs revealed through a local labour force or manpower survey.

It is probably true, however, that a further education funded on student numbers, retention, and success, is likely to be more attentive to its users' needs. But some needs are more expensive to satisfy than others. Provision for occupational training requiring sophisticated equipment or specialist materials, or for seriously physically handicapped students, for example, is obviously going to be more expensive.

Further recognition may be given to the extra expense of providing a curriculum for socially and educationally excluded groups, but it could also be the case that a ceiling is placed on the amount of public expenditure that any one individual may receive - for example, for students who conspicuously fail examination after examination. The European Commission for Research, Education and Training is concerned to combat the exclusion of groups, such as the unemployed, from life-long education and access to information technology, and action on exclusion is likely to form the basis of future equal opportunity policy (see p.35).

The curriculum response to equality of opportunity and policies aimed at encouraging social integration and combating exclusion is complex. In future, more effort is likely to be spent on recruiting excluded groups, on taking courses to the places they frequent, on offering a bridging curriculum between group cultural aspiration and official economically-determined learning objectives, on adapting and making available more user-friendly information technology, and on providing more widespread, effective, and intensive tuition in basic skills, such as literacy and numeracy. These developments will be integrated with others to help create a more comprehensive curriculum framework.

Partnerships

Libertarian educationalists opposed to compulsory schooling have long observed that education is conceived in 19th-century social·class terms as an institution *imposed* on the mass of the population for their own or the nation's good. It is education *for* the people, but not *of* the people.

For the last fifteen years, the aims of further education have gradually been refashioned to make it subservient to industry, with the vocational curriculum being largely determined by employers. The relationship of colleges and the further education curriculum to four influential groups - the government (including FEFC and TECs), employers, universities, and student users - remains unstable and problematic. In what way, to what extent, and in what proportion should the curriculum be controlled and determined and by whom?

One solution is to involve a wide range of employers and community groups in deciding what colleges are to offer, in effect, to promise educational resources to individuals and groups external to the institution and to work with them in deciding, planning, and recruiting for those courses. Not only might such a policy improve participation rates, but it is need-sensitive in a way that traditional supply-led educational provision never was. Moreover, it avoids the problem of imposing traditional high-cultural forms of education on groups that are unlikely either to seek or to benefit from such an exposure. The rhetoric of partnership also helps to obscure the relationship between funder, provider, and beneficiary. The issue of who is to pay for education and training - the government, employers, or individuals - remains for the time being unanswered.

Given the present inequalities in personal and family income, mass further education cannot be sustained on the basis of students', or their families', payment of fees. Neither does the complex quasi-market, based on the Funding Council's funding methodology, seem able to sustain an equitable distribution of education and training facilities, responsive to local need and sustaining more expensive or minority provision, although it is probably too soon to pass judgement on a system so recently introduced. A method of learning credits or vouchers with a reclaimable money value and distributed to individuals to *buy* the service would have similar drawbacks, be more cumbersome, and (because it would not so readily be able to take into account marginal costs) be more costly.

More fundamentally, the existing funding methodology and the voucher proposals have been justified as a means of extending choice and leverage to students as customers or consumers. In practice, however, these approaches do not deal effectively with the question of power over, and partnership in deciding, the curriculum. Students, like shoppers, would only have power as individual customers, and any mass exercise of purchasing power would be blind in intention and to social outcome. There is no free or quasi-market substitute for purposeful decision-making and planned partnerships to achieve mutually desirable educational goals.

The present chaotic system of vocational qualifications and awards, heavily biased towards short-term skill acquisition at the expense of knowledge, theory, and values, is unsatisfactory, in terms both of the inadequacy of its content and of its waste of human potential. The divide between academic and vocational education has to be closed. The need for lifelong education for the whole population - not merely for the workforce - has to be recognised as does the importance of moral, cultural, aesthetic, social, scientific, and recreational education. These aims will only be achieved by curtailing the short-term expressions of self-interest of industry, professional bodies, and universities, and their power over the further education sector.

What is required is an extension of partnership approaches so that the interests of individuals students, social categories, and the social community as a whole, are taken into account alongside those of other vested interests, with radical modification to existing systems of funding and charging. The concept of stake holding is a property-orientated version of partnership commitment. Partnerships based on equality and fashioned for a common purpose have the potential to form the backbone of an emergent *community* further education.

The partnership approach to further education results in greater participation, more equality of opportunity, and a significant shift in curriculum content towards one based on popular culture and perceived by users to have economic and social relevance. More education partnerships may be predicted to develop in further education, possibly through extending franchising arrangements, with the curriculum responding more closely to individual, community, and employer need.

Systems

The increasing numbers of students attracted by open access and equality of opportunity policies make greater demands on college management and organisation. New and more systematic methods for delivering the curriculum are replacing the older tradition of the professional lecturer working individually and independently with a group of students in a classroom, studio, or workshop. The various activities involved in taking a person through an education and training process to successful culmination are separated conceptually, refined, and recombined as a *process* or organisational *cycle*. Further education is seen as having various inputs leading to a series of interactions which result in a measurable output, expressed, for example, in terms of qualifications gained, *added educational value*, or people educated or skilled to a specified level.

Organisational thinking in terms of cycles or systems, aimed at achieving a mass throughput of students to a time schedule, is not new to a further education with a tradition of industrial training, but another powerful paradigm of teaching as a craft practised by an independent school master passing on skills to scholar apprentices is rapidly being displaced by the concept of a staged process of continuous mass delivery of education and training facilities by teams of specialists. The effects of idiosyncratic individual teacher performance are minimised as colleges struggle to ensure consistency of service and output through the installation of monitoring and quality systems. The cyclical nature of curriculum thinking is encapsulated in the idea of monitoring student or teacher performance against various indicators (recruitment, attendance, retention, achievement), which leads to action being taken to improve performance or output *the next time round*. Table 10.1 demonstrates one possible way of representing the modern further education curriculum cycle.

Table 10.1

The further education curriculum cycle

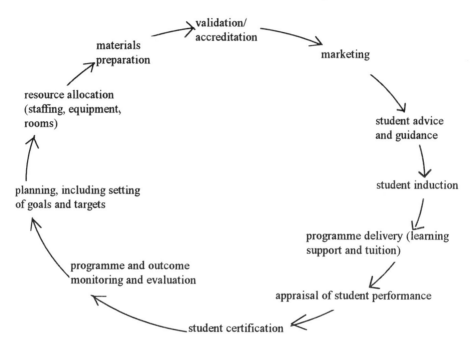

Systems thinking, accompanied by more and more detailed assessment of the efficiency and effectiveness of the curriculum, is increasingly apparent in all discussion of further education management. Yet, curiously, the training of staff and their contractual conditions (they are for example, still separated into two categories: teachers and support workers), together with actual practice which remains very traditional in many colleges, lag behind the external pressures for introducing new, effective, and efficient systems.

Nevertheless, in all discussion of curriculum planning, the impact of the management approach to mass provision is manifest in discussion of staffing costs, student group size, qualification aims, the number of *guided learning hours* allocated for a programme, retention, and achievement. Cost weighting factors for subject areas increasingly determine whether courses in those subjects are offered or closed.

Progression

Another important feature of the new further education curriculum is the emphasis placed on progression, skill enhancement, attainment and attainment level, and successful mass throughput. Essentially, the further education curriculum is seen as a complicated machine for rapidly racheting up the industrial and commercial skill levels of the workforce. It is no longer (if it ever was) a selection of knowledge made available to the adult population for their intellectual enlightenment and interest - to be sampled as and when they so decide.

The new further education curriculum has had imposed upon it - almost like a slave branded with a branding iron - a framework or grid of levels - the NVQ framework (see Chapter Six). Simultaneously, the government, through the National Advisory Council for Education and Training Targets, has set targets, expressed in terms of these levels, against which to assess progress made in raising the amount and level of the workforce's skills and qualifications.

A college would need to review its curriculum against the NVQ grid, each major subject area being examined horizontally, in terms of the comprehensiveness of programme provision, and vertically, in terms of its range and succession of level. Students might expect and colleges might benefit from a full coverage of the framework. From this exercise, a curriculum map, indicating entry and exit points and routes of progression, might be developed to assist both students and staff in understanding and negotiating the local topography of the curriculum and thus ensuring the requisite degree of progression.

At present, college curricula are beset with major discontinuities and gaps in provision which limit student choice, deter natural progression, result in course duplication, and incur unnecessary costs. There is general agreement that the traditional divisions between academic, vocational, and practical craft courses, and vocational and non-vocational provision, have to be eliminated and that further thought has to be given to the relationship between company-based and college-based commercial and industrial training.

Under the FEFC funding methodology, colleges are allocated resources against the value of qualifications that contribute towards raising skill levels, with a further cost-weighting factor, relating to the actual estimated cost of delivery, encouraging or discouraging the provision of particular subjects, for example, business and finance, dental hygiene, animal husbandry or building design.

The insistence that every student must pursue a qualification aim accredited by a body external to the college results in the concept of progression permeating the whole curriculum. Funding of students is dependent on their pursuing agreed qualification aims, with a further payment dependent on the qualification being achieved. The retention and achievement of students is also rewarded by the funding mechanism, contributing, yet again, to the emphasis placed on student progression (see pp.67-9).

Accreditation

With each learning programme possessing at least one recognised qualification aim, towards which students must strive, all separable parts of the curriculum must become accredited. The Funding Council does not fund study without a specifically-stated qualification aim - which from 1996 must be more than a college certificate. Unless an alternative source of funding can be found, any course without recognised accreditation will disappear from the curriculum.

The effect on former recreational course provision has already been devastating. Users find difficulty in grasping that traditional further education subjects such as dress making, pottery, sculpture, drama, music, creative writing, public speaking, and ballroom dancing have value only in as much as they result in a qualification. For many the intrinsic value of the programme is justification enough for study, but that intrinsic value does not bring funding with it.

In industry, workers demonstrate their skills directly on the job. Their skills are not demonstrated by the exhibition of qualifications or certificates, but in successful performance and achievement. In the vocational curriculum, the absurdity of elevating the qualification over the actual skill performance is dealt with by matching the qualification as closely as possible to particular competence elements. The qualification becomes nothing more nor less than a statement that an individual can perform certain specified skills in a standard setting to a given level, effectively the aim of the NVQ.

Colleges have been faced with the immense task of seeking accreditation for all courses not seen as having qualification aims recognised for funding purposes by the FEFC, or having to close large areas of the traditional curriculum. They are achieving this task by devoting more resources to accreditation, either by seeking out for adoption accredited courses already in existence elsewhere, or by mounting large-scale accreditation exercises involving examination boards and, possibly, the development of internal systems of validation.

Some areas of the traditional further education curriculum have suffered from a surfeit of qualifications, with examination boards competing to provide alternative forms of accreditation, while in other areas there has been a conspicuous failure to develop any appropriate qualifications or to keep up with the rapidly changing demands of industry and technology for new skills.

The process of accreditation is also closely related to the business of ensuring student progression and of curriculum mapping. A number of the curriculum concepts originally developed for organising higher education courses and found, for example, in advanced form in the American Community Colleges and the British university sector are beginning to impact on further education. One approach to curriculum organisation is that of the *unitised* or *modular* curriculum consisting of interchangeable course *bricks* that can be chosen and assembled into different structures according to requirement. Each unit or module is given a credit weighting related to its length or level, with students being allowed to gather credits at their own pace towards a major award. Institutions, mostly of higher education, adopting this approach have developed elaborate systems for the recognition of and the establishment of parity between their units and credits, known as CATS - Credit Accumulation and Transfer Schemes (see Chapter Six).

The complexity of further education, especially the varying lengths of courses (usually determined by independent external examination boards) and the predominantly part-time mode of study has made it difficult to transfer these methods of unitisation and accreditation directly, but the further education future is undoubtedly one of standardising and simplifying accreditation systems.

For the moment, the process of undertaking universal accreditation dominates the further education curriculum, placing a new and insistent emphasis on measuring what students have learned, methods of assessment, and the comparability of student performance and qualifications. Accreditation is inextricably related to funding and questions of efficiency: how can a qualification of a particular kind be achieved at least cost to the organisation? The new curriculum is an accredited curriculum: more than ever before it is output-related, the outputs being quantified in the form of qualifications - symbolic tokens of students' levels of knowledge, skill, competence, or achievement.

Competence

The provision of technical or vocational education is the quintessential feature of traditional further education. Further education colleges have prided themselves on their ability to serve industry and commerce by assisting in the training of technologists, technicians, and craftspeople.

From the Second World War for thirty-five years, colleges worked in partnership with industry to create day-release, sandwich, and other courses, combining learning on the job with college-based study. Knowledge, skills, and work values were learned partly on the job and partly in college classrooms and workshops. Further education has a long history of providing practical, employment-orientated skill training acceptable to employers.

The exposure of the further education curriculum to the industrial demands of, for example, the engineering and construction industries, has predisposed it to the technique of subdividing tasks into their simplest component parts and then assembling them, not only to simulate or perform the productive act, but in the belief that this was the most effective way to train the workforce in the skills required.

In many areas of the further education curriculum serving industry, students spent time in workshops learning the processes they needed to perform in the course of their work. They often made use of a series of work sheets, working from simpler to more complex designs. In classrooms and laboratory situations, where additional background knowledge and theory were imparted, lessons were similarly structured, using the same curriculum assembly model. The aim was to achieve as efficiently as possible the requisite level of skill among trainees.

The National Council for Vocational Qualifications built on this technical foundation by undertaking the task of developing standards of occupational *competence* and ensuring vocational qualifications were based on them. National Vocational Qualifications are said to be competence-based, that is, based on a *statement of competence,* incorporating standards determined by employers' representatives responsible for maintaining those standards. An

NVQ is intended to incorporate an assessment of performance to a specified standard, in addition to an assessment of the knowledge and understanding required to underpin or extend the performance (NCVQ, 1988a, p.14). In trying to open up access to qualifications, the National Council also insists that NVQs should be independent of the mode of learning, unrestricted as to methods and periods of learning and age barriers.

While colleges are seen as providers of NVQs, this kind of qualification, being mode-free, can be offered wherever vocational education and training is going on - in company training departments and training agencies. The key value, continually underscored by the government and the National Council, is the relevance of the qualification to industrial requirements: its basis on the ability to perform in employment. This is what *competence* was originally intended to signify.

While finding a sympathetic niche in further education departments accustomed to providing practically-based courses for industry, the competence approach has met with a mixed response from a workforce delivering a complex *multiform* curriculum with both academic and vocational traditions. It has been criticised in academic quarters for failing to give sufficient recognition to the importance of knowledge acquisition (FEFC 1994b, Hodkinson and Issitt, 1995, Hyland, 1994). But its overall long-term effects on a further education curriculum already orientated in large part to meeting the needs of industry are immense.

At a very general level, competence translates as *know-how* (in contrast to *knowing that*), with the consequence that the further education curriculum becomes focused on the business of skill development and its appraisal. As already mentioned, this is nothing new to further education, but in technical subjects the value may become monolithic, leading to an even greater emphasis being placed on the performance of practical tasks, possibly at the expense of knowledge and theory. But the ethos of competence also begins to permeate more academically-orientated disciplines, leading them, too, to formulate their aims in terms of behavioural objectives, the acquisition of academic skills, or projects involving *doing*. A paper commissioned by the Employment Department's Methods Strategy Unit asserted the possibility of developing occupational standards for roles at level five of NVQ - in spite of difficulties in incorporating knowledge, understanding, and values (Employment Department, 1993a).

In 1991, the Government announced plans for a new qualification, a General National Vocational Qualification (GNVQ), to operate in parallel with NVQ. Together with NVQ, the GNVQ was intended to replace other vocational qualifications and to become the main national means for providing vocational education and training. Another objective was to make available an alternative qualification (of comparable standard) to GCE A level for students staying on in full-time education beyond the age of 16. GNVQs are intended to give a *broad-based* vocational education providing students with the opportunity not only to learn *core* skills but to acquire the knowledge underpinning a vocational area. The aim is to combine vocational attainment with academic achievement as a foundation from which students can progress either to higher education or to employment. By 1995, Foundation, Intermediate, and Advanced GNVQs were available in fourteen areas, including business, health and social care, manufacturing, engineering, and information technology.

Unlike NVQ, the award of the GNVQ does not imply that a student can perform *competently* in an occupation immediately on qualifying. The widespread adoption of GNVQ qualifications in further education, however, does indicate the growing influence on the curriculum of the competence approach and the perceived requirement for occupational relevance. While this influence has been maligned in academic quarters, it is worth pointing out that much of the former academic curriculum substance - general education, preparation for higher education, vocational and higher education - had little appeal, relevance, or application for many students in further education. The emerging synthesis of academic and vocational education, assisted by the catalyst of the concept of competence, appears to be contributing positively to the accessibility of the further education curriculum.

Adoption of the competence approach, however, is not the only way in which the further education curriculum may retain its relevance to the economy. Other more radical linkages are possible. Further education colleges could play a much more direct role in economic regeneration by embarking on partnership projects with local firms and community groups to rebuild and re-equip industrial plant and commercial and community property, while, at the same time, providing skill training, jobs, and eventually secure employment (see Wymer, 1995).

Learning-centredness

Learning-centredness is not the same thing as student-centredness. If the student users of further education were paramount, the curriculum would be organised in a radically different way from its present *dissociative* form, and without the confusing complexity of hundreds of accrediting bodies. What is clearly apparent is that further education does not have a streamlined, national, integrated curriculum based on a genuine analysis of students' interests, learning needs, and vocational aspirations. Indeed, it has been argued that many emergent features of the further education curriculum, for example, the weight given to advice, guidance and counselling, and the growing requirement for additional support, are a direct consequence of its apparent inability to serve its student users in any rational way (see Chapter Nine).

Yet colleges, under pressure to increase student numbers in the face of competition from other providers, have been forced to become more market or user conscious. Colleges undertake needs analyses, make use of workforce data, conduct marketing campaigns, and engage in public relations and image enhancement. The curriculum has to be presented in such a way as to attract (voluntarily) customers or *consumers*.

This market context of consumer choice may have some bearing on, but does not satisfactorily explain, the recent profound shift of paradigm in the further education curriculum - reflected in changes in terminology - from *teaching* to *learning*. Suddenly, the symmetrical relationship assumed to exist between teaching and learning seems to have been tipped heavily in favour of learning. The teacher does not so much teach as provide support on request to the individual seeking to learn (see Reeves, 1995).

The change is probably best understood as a response to two interrelated factors: pressure to reduce costs and the increasing availability of information technology for educational applications. If a large measure of responsibility for an adult's education can be moved from the teacher to the student, making the student an *auto-didact*, then the amount of teacher time spent with that student might be reduced or spent more purposefully in giving guidance to the student on how she might acquire the study skills to learn unaided. Teacher time is the most expensive component of contemporary, labour-intensive, college provision. There are striking parallels here with the spread of the practice of self-service at petrol stations and in supermarkets, and with the government's

Care in the Community policy, which transfers responsibility for older people, the infirm and sick, from state-run establishments to the *community*. The new self-taught student can be provided with technological aids in the form of access to computerised library facilities and computerised teaching materials.

Learning-centred approaches to the curriculum are reflected in the organisation of colleges, by the development and spread of learning or resource centres. These are suites, open for long hours and equipped with learning and reference materials (paper-based, audio-visual, and/or electronic), where students, separately or in groups, may work to a study plan. Tutors help plan the students' schedules and conduct individual or group tutorials to support students in their work and to ensure they achieve their learning goals.

Study can be undertaken at a time convenient to the student, there is less dependence on the presence of a tutor, and restrictions imposed by the need for an economy of group size are removed. For these reasons, the learning centre system is seen as having distinct advantages over the traditional class of lecturer and students attending at a set time and place. Doubts as to the appropriateness of learning centres for students with learning difficulties, for example, with poor levels of literacy, have been expressed, but, paradoxically, the approach has already been widely adopted for basic skills, the provision of additional support, and unemployed groups.

Those defending traditional classroom methods against the tide of learning centre conversions have made much of the need for group support and facilitation, while conveniently ignoring the failure of the older system to deal with individual differences in student learning requirements, learning speed, and learning preference. But group learning methods - as opposed to group teaching methods - can also be made available in learning centres. There is evidence of spontaneously-generated group work in many learning centres, with students co-operating in solving their study problems. The possibilities for systematic college organisation of peer group learning support groups and networks have yet to be fully explored.

Supported by information technology, caseloading (teachers allocated a number of students), and peer group support groups, learning centres are likely to have an increasing impact on the form and delivery of the further education curriculum.

Specialisation

The expansion of student numbers and the need for systems of mass delivery inevitably result in a growing division of labour and specialisation of curriculum and staffing function. These trends are accompanied by a realisation of the choices and economies afforded by scale.

Most colleges provide a wide-ranging and varied curriculum at entry and NVQ 1 and 2 levels, but at higher levels the range of subject and vocational area will be more limited as a consequence of the investment required in staff expertise, capital equipment, and customised premises. Colleges are likely to specialise in vocational areas and related qualifications, ensuring comprehensive provision only at a regional level.

Specialisation is also apparent in the development of distinct curriculum functions and curriculum expertise. One important division of labour is between the *writers and producers* of high-quality learning packages in paper or electronic form and *learning facilitators* (formerly tutors) whose job is to help students access the packaged learning materials used in learning centres. Requiring considerable investment to produce, many of the packages will have to be bought in by colleges, leaving college staff with the work of undertaking the tutoring. Other emergent curriculum specialisms include student advice and guidance, basic skills and additional support tuition, learning assistance, computer-assisted learning expertise, quality assurance, accreditation and validation work, marketing, franchise/partnership and outreach organisation, and work-experience supervision. The future further education curriculum will be supported by differently-graded specialists, each undertaking an essential function in the curriculum cycle.

Products and packages

The learning centre approach, together with the divergent functions of expert course material production on the one hand and tuition or guided learning support on the other, has resulted in renewed interest being shown in the concept of the curriculum as a package of learning materials or *product* line.

For more than 25 years, the Open University has delivered a carefully-staged higher education curriculum consisting of courses sub-divided into sequences of blocks and units. Primary materials consist of quality printed booklets supported by a combination of television programmes, tape recordings, set text books, supplementary materials, and assignments and, in the case of science and technology courses, experiment kits and computer exercises. Students study this packaged learning in their own time, but are allocated tutors and counsellors and the opportunity to attend tutorials and counselling sessions. Some courses require students to attend an intensive residential week of study - or summer school.

The Open University has long provided a distinctive model of curriculum delivery which, in the 1980s, was to have been applied by the Open College to vocational education and training. There is now a growing demand for quality student learning materials for further education and new possibilities for combining them with the recent advances and availability of information technology.

In future, it is likely that each student will be exposed to a multi-media package of carefully prepared and integrated learning materials, which she will study in her own time, possibly in a learning centre or at home. The student's progress will be supported and monitored by a tutor or learning support worker, perhaps with pay related to case load or individual students' continuing study or achievement. Students will be able to select a variety of learning blocks (modules) or units from a curriculum catalogue or menu. Units may be added or combined to allow for accreditation recorded in the form of a profile or record of achievement - much like an itemised receipt at a supermarket check-out counter.

The development of open learning products, however, will be limited by economies of scale. Quality materials - printed, electronic, video, and tape recording - are expensive to develop and to keep updated. Sizeable development costs will be incurred prior to delivery and the product will need a large market to be viable. It is debatable whether individual colleges will have the resources to develop a range of courses in-house. Many products are likely to be bought in and customised to local requirements.

The product approach has the additional advantage of ensuring consistency in the delivery of the curriculum. It constitutes a move from small-scale idiosyncratic individual production of the curriculum, dependent on the skill of the teacher, to mass standardised collective production, with quality very much a function of investment in expertise.

Automation

Until recently, a teacher's main tools were chalk, board, pen, and textbooks. Science teachers had a more complex tool box with test tubes, microscopes, scientific instruments, and experimental equipment. Art, wood work, metal work, geography, and physical education teachers also had their own specialities, but compared with the average factory, educational institutions were generally destitute of equipment to aid the education process.

Further education was different in that in subjects, such as engineering, foundry work, construction, and catering, there were workshops, or the like, where industrial processes were engaged in or simulated. The equipment made available, however, was the kind used in particular industrial processes and was not designed especially for educational purposes.

From the 1960s, the tools of chalk and board were gradually supplemented by machinery. Typewriters, roneo and xerox machines, and then photocopiers, which allowed educational materials to be duplicated, overhead projectors which displayed diagrams on acetate to the class, tape recorders, slide and film projectors, and then television and video recordings, became more widely available, providing the teacher with a range of *audio-visual aids.*

In the last ten years, however, colleges have been able to access and make more and better use of information technology. Computers, coupled with telecommunication techniques, make possible the systematic processing of large quantities of information at tremendous speed and its almost simultaneous dissemination across large distances. The widespread and increasing application of information technology is in evidence across a broad spectrum of the further education curriculum, with nearly every vocational area recognising the importance of computer applications.

In the 1960s, attempts were made in America to develop teaching machines but now, for the first time, the possibility exists for the automation - or control - of the learning process to reduce or dispense with the role of the traditional teacher. The learning centre approach mentioned above is being combined with computers and telecommunications to produce a new concept of flexible and distance learning.

Anywhere in the world, theoretically, a student at a networked computer terminal can receive in electronic form a learning package and communicate with a tutor about its content. Shortly, communications will be possible in multi-media form: written, visual, and aural. This facility will immeasurably enhance the existing limited kinds of computer-assisted learning, and give people much greater access to learning materials in their own homes.

It is forecast that, in the next ten years, nearly every home in the United Kingdom will possess a machine combining the functions of television, computer, video, music centre, telephone, fax, clock, and printer. Auxiliary equipment, such as virtual reality facilities, games, and security alarms, will also be available. While, initially, the equipment will be used for communications, entertainment, and recreation, in the longer term, it is envisaged that it will also play a major educational role. If colleges are to have a significant involvement in providing computer-assisted learning, they will need to invest heavily in the production of suitable materials (see Chapter Eight).

The effect of the information revolution and the speed of its impact on the further education curriculum are difficult to foresee. Some futurologists are forecasting that the college, in any traditionally recognisable form, will disappear. Colleges may survive as production and editing centres for multi-media curriculum packages, as skill assessment and registration networks, as skill training centres for those skills that cannot be learned through virtual reality techniques, or as vast therapy centres for people - many computer dyslexic - unable or unwilling to participate in the European learning society.

Developments in information technology will transform the further education curriculum. They appear to have a vast potential for assisting in the drive for mass life-long participation in educational activity. Much depends on investment in developing materials comparable in quality with the best produced for entertainment and recreational purposes, but there is, at present, little to indicate that government or media companies are prepared to invest in educational information technology at the level required.

* * * * * * * *

The characteristics described above are mutually reinforcing and will eventually result in a more unified and distinctive further education curriculum. The residual and dissociative elements mentioned in earlier chapters are still distinguishable but, if the further education sector is to succeed in performing the gargantuan task expected of it, its objectives of improving the education and training levels of the post-16 population in the context of life-long learning will have to be pursued with greater self confidence, renewed vigour, and a clearer awareness of possible strategy. All remaining social-class-derived and exclusive anachronisms, including the academic/vocational divide, must be removed to create a mass, comprehensive, non-selective, student-centred curriculum, based on partnerships, and guaranteeing a greater equality of educational opportunity for all. Let no-one continue to doubt the existence of a viable and identifiable further education. We, in further education, commit ourselves to fashioning a curriculum to serve, not merely the interests of state, employer, or university, but each individual's needs and aspirations.

Postscript

As this book went to press, reports on the content of the government-commissioned review of the 16-to-19 curriculum, to be published in Spring 1996, appeared in *The Guardian* (2.3.96) and *Times Educational Supplement* (1.3.96).

Sir Ron Dearing, the government's curriculum adviser, is expected to propose that existing academic and vocational qualifications (GCE A levels, GCSEs, GNVQs and NVQs) are retained but related more closely within a strengthened and more coherent framework of national awards. In line with Conservative commitments, the dilution of GCE A level standards will be prevented, possibly by limiting the proportion of young people sitting A levels. A series of measures will be taken to improve the status of vocational and practical courses: GNVQs will be renamed *Applied A levels*, academic and vocational awarding bodies may be merged, and attempts made to relaunch Youth Training with Youth Traineeships.

Young people between 16 and 19 will be able to follow three routes: the *academic* (through GCSE and GCE A level), the *applied* (through GNVQ Intermediate and Advanced), and the *practical* (through job-specific NVQs). The first and second routes would be pursued in the main by students in schools or colleges, while the third would be available for those in employment or in Youth Traineeships. As individuals progressed through four levels - Entry, Foundation, Intermediate, and Advanced - they would be able to change routes and combine elements of academic, applied, and practical study.

Other recommendations are said to be:

- an Advanced National Diploma awarded for two A levels or the vocational equivalent.

- an Intermediate National Diploma for five GCSE grade Cs or equivalent.

- a National General Diploma at age 18, similar to the baccalaureat, and covering four areas of study: - (i) mathematics, science and technology, (ii) modern languages, (iii) arts and humanities, and (iv) *the way the world works* (with business and economics).

- a reduction in the number of GCE A level syllabuses.

- a relaunch of Youth Training with Youth Traineeships.

- a relaunch of the National Record of Achievement as a *lifelong learning planner*.

- more rigorous GNVQs with less cumbersome assessment.

- a new GCE A/S level taken as the first half of an A level course (to encourage breadth and to reduce drop-out).

- a revival of S level to stretch the brightest candidates.

(as reported in *The Guardian*, 2.3.96).

Donald MacLeod, the *Guardian's* education correspondent, described the plan as bold and "designed to build on present qualifications and courses rather than calling for a return to square one". It is intended that the present confused jungle of qualifications be shaped into a system of national awards to raise the status of vocational courses, improve retention rates, and increase student choice across academic and applied courses (*Guardian*, 2.3.96, p.4).

Dearing's actual report awaits publication, but it is already apparent that the archaic distinctions between academic, technical (applied), and practical forms of the curriculum (once institutionalised in the form of grammar, technical high, and secondary modern schools, and deriving from deep-rooted social-class and occupational divisions) are to continue. They will be justified on the grounds that "stability is important" - the same stability, of course, which has led to the education system's failure to keep pace with international competition.

While efforts to raise the status of applied and practical routes are laudable, their success is likely to prove illusory against the backcloth of underlying social-class reality. The proposal for a facility for individuals to combine academic, applied, and practical elements is, in fact, a recognition that the present organisation of the curriculum renders this impossible. Given the comparative status of the elements, however, would students actually make such choices and would institutions be able to offer the requisite range of courses?

Dearing is also concerned about the 20 per cent of young people leaving school with no GCSE passes. He proposes national awards at *entry* level, probably to be taken at further education colleges. Fourteen-year-olds could leave school and take courses at colleges which, he believes, have expertise in providing for learners who were unsuccessful at school. Some colleges, of course, already have schemes for pre-16s who could not come to terms with school. But the likely effect will be one of confirming the segregated *academic* role of the secondary school and the *practical* route to which the young people in question are most likely to be confined.

A fundamental question for further education is the extent to which the implementation of proposals intended for 16-to-19-year-olds will affect a curriculum that provides mainly for adults. The *juvenescence* of the further education curriculum - its use of content and qualifications devised with a younger age group in mind than the adults who receive it - has already been remarked upon. It is nevertheless worrying that the context for which the framework of awards is proposed does not appear to be one of a lifelong further education, in which the dominant mode would be that of part-time study combined with the business of being a citizen (with or without employment).

The Dearing report constitutes a particular official expression of the general ideas already dominating and shaping the further education curriculum and described in Chapter Ten. Dearing is concerned with increasing participation, raising standards, student choice, curriculum breadth, vocational preparation, comparability of qualifications, and a coherent, simplified system of delivery, but not with equality of opportunity or outcome. If implemented, his proposals will reinforce further education's historically *dissociative* curriculum.

Abbreviations and Acronyms

AEB	Associated Examining Board
AfC	Association for Colleges
ALBSU	Adult Literacy and Basic Skills Unit
AMSPAR	Association of Medical Secretaries, Practice Administrators and Receptionists
APL	Accreditation of Prior Learning
ATCs	Adult Training Centres
BSA	Basic Skills Agency
BTEC	Business and Technology Education Council
CATS	Credit Accumulation and Transfer Scheme (or System)
CCASA	Community College Association of South Africa
CEF	Colleges' Employers' Forum
CGLI	City and Guilds of London Institute
CNAA	Council for National Academic Awards
CRE	Commission for Racial Equality
CRET	Commission for Research, Education and Training (European Union)
CSC	College Sector Coalition
DE	Department of Employment
DfEE	Department for Education and Employment
DfE	Department for Education
DES	Department of Education and Science
EO&C	Equal Opportunities and Conferences
Ed	Edited
ESF	European Social Fund
ESOL	English for Speakers of Other Languages
FE	Further Education
FECG	Further Education Campaign Group
FEFC	Further Education Funding Council
FHEA	Further and Higher Education Act
GCE	General Certificate of Education
GCE A level	General Certificate of Education Advanced Level
GCSE	General Certificate of Secondary Education
GNVQ	General National Vocational Qualification
HE	Higher Education
HMSO	Her Majesty's Stationery Office
IT	Information Technology

LAMDA	London Academy of Music and Dramatic Art
LCCI	London Chamber of Commerce and Industry
LEA	Local Education Authority
MSC	Manpower Services Commission
NACETT	National Advisory Council for Education and Training Targets
NAMSS	National Association for Managers of Students Services
NCVQ	National Council for Vocational Qualifications
NFER	National Foundation for Educational Research
NIACE	National Institute of Adult Continuing Education
NICE	National Institute of Continuing Education
NOCN	National Open College Network
n.p.	no page number
NRA	National Record of Achievement
NTETs	National Targets for Education and Training
NVQ	National Vocational Qualifications
OBA	Own Brand Award (by Awarding Bodies)
ONC	Ordinary National Certificate
OND	Ordinary National Diploma
OPCS	Office of Population Censuses and Surveys
PCFC	Polytechnics and Colleges Funding Council
PGCE	Post Graduate Certificate of Education
QUANGO	Quasi-autonomous non-governmental organisation
REPLAN	A programme sponspored by the Department of Education and Science and Welsh Office to improve the educational opportunities available to unemployed adults.
RSA	Royal Society of Arts
RSG	Rate Support Grant
RVQ	Review of Vocational Qualifications
SSR	Staff-Student Ratio
SVQs	Scottish Vocational Qualifications
TDLB	Training and Development Lead Body
TECs	Training and Enterprise Councils
TVEI	Technical and Vocational Education Initiative
WEA	Workers' Educational Assocation
WFTE	Weighted Full-Time Equivalent (students)
WMT	West Midlands Travel
YOPS	Youth Opportunities Scheme
YTS	Youth Training Scheme

References and bibliography

ALBSU (1992), *Basic Skills in Further Education Colleges,* London, ALBSU.

Anderson, H. (1995), *Disabled People and the Labour Market,* Birmingham, West Midlands Low Pay Unit.

Association for Colleges (1994 Nov), *A Curriculum for Colleges, a policy paper,* London, AfC.

Association for Colleges (1995 May), *A Manifesto for Further Education,* London, AfC.

Association for Colleges (1995), *Further into the Future, Annual Report, 1994,* London, AfC.

Ball, W. (1987), *Post-Sixteen Education and the Promotion of Equal Opportunities: A Case Study of Policies and Provision in One Local Authority,* Policy Paper in Ethnic Relations, No. 8, Warwick, Centre for Research in Ethnic Relations.

Barnard, H.C. (1961), *A History of English Education from 1760,* London, University of London Press.

Bernstein, B. (1973), *Class, Codes and Control,* St Albans, Paladin.

Bilston Community College (1986), *Culture, Race and Education: The Views of Afro-Caribbean, Asian, and White Further Education Students,* Bilston Equal Rights and Opportunities Development Unit.

Bilston Community College (1994), *Agreement on staff working at weekends,* Bilston, BCC.

Bilston Community College (1994), *Contract of Employment for Management Spine Staff appointed or promoted after 1 April 1994,* Bilston, BCC.

Birmingham City Council (1995), *Discussing CATS, Making a case for the development of a regional credit accumulation and transfer initiative*, Birmingham, BCC.

Bristow, A. (1970), *Inside the colleges of Further Education*, London, HMSO.

Calder, J., McCollum, A., Morgan, A., and Thorpe, M. (1995), *Learning Effectiveness of Open and Flexible Learning in Vocational Education*, Department for Education and Employment, Research Series No. 58, London, DfEE.

Cantor, L.M. and Roberts I.F. (1986), *Further Education Today, A Critical Review* (Third Edition), London, Routledge and Kegan Paul.

Carey, N. (1996), Telling FE's Fortune, *FE Now*, New Year, 1996.

Carter, M.P. (1963), *Education, Employment and Leisure*, Oxford, Pergamon.

Central Statistical Office (1995), *Social Trends 25*, 1995 Edition, London, HMSO.

Chitty, C. (ed.) (1991), *Post-16 Education Studies in Access and Achievement*, London, Kogan Page.

City and Guilds of London Institute (1993), *A Short History, 1878-1992*, London, C&GLI.

Cockburn, C. (1987), *Two-Track Training, Sex Inequalities and the YTS*, London, Macmillan.

Colleges' Employers' Forum (1993), *Consultation Conference*, (11.11.1993), Colleges' Employers' Forum Bulletin (No. 90), London, CEF.

Colleges' Employers' Forum (1995), *Case-Loading in Action, College Case Studies*, Occasional Paper 95/5, London, CEF.

Commission for Racial Equality (1982), *Further Education in a Multi-Racial Society: A Policy Report*, London, CRE.

Crowley-Bainton, T. (1995), *Evaluation of the Open Learning Credits Pilot Programme,* Department for Education and Employment Research Series No. 45, Sheffield, Employment Department.

Curzon, L. B. (1976), *Teaching in Further Education,* (third edition), London, Holt, Rinehart and Winston.

Dean, A. (1984), *Further Education Provision for Students with Severe Learning Difficulties - Analysis of Survey Findings,* pp. 5-9, in Dean, A. and Hegarty, S., op. cit.

Dean, A. and Hegarty, S. (eds) (1984), *Learning for Independence: Post-16 Educational Provision for People with Severe Learning Difficulties,* London, FEU.

Dearing, R. (1995), *Review of 16-19 Qualifications, Interim Report,* London, no publisher.

Dennison, B. and Kirk, R. (1990), *Do, Review, Learn, Apply: A Simple Guide to Experiential Learning,* Oxford, Blackwell Educational.

Department for Education (1992), *National Education and Training Targets,* Fact Pack, London, DfE.

Department for Education (1995), *Statistics of Education: Students in Further and Higher Education, in former polytechnics, former PCFC establishments and colleges in the FE Sector, 1993-94,* Department for Education, Government Statistical Services.

Department for Education and Employment, the Scottish Office, and Welsh Office (1995), *Lifetime Learning, a consultation document,* London, DfEE.

Department of Education and Science (1966), *A Plan for Polytechnics and other Colleges,* London, HMSO.

Department of Education and Science and Welsh Office (1987), *Managing Colleges Efficiently. Report of a Study of Efficiency in Non-advanced Further Education for the Government and the Local Authority Associations,* London, HMSO.

Department of Education and Science (1988a), *Education Reform Act 1988, Government of Maintained Further and Higher Education Colleges* (Circular 8/88) London, DES.

Department of Education and Science (1988b), *Education Reform Act 1988, local management of further and higher education colleges: planning and delegation schemes and articles of government* (Circular 9/88), London, DES.

Department of Education and Science (1989), *Students with Special Needs in Further Education, Education Observed, Her Majesty's Inspectorate*, London, HMSO.

Department of Education and Science and Welsh Office (1991), *Education and Training for the 21st Century*, Vols 1 and 2, London, HMSO.

Department of Education and Science, Department of Employment, and Welsh Office (1991), *Education and Training for the 21st Century*, Vols 1 and 2, (Command 1536, May 1991), London, HMSO.

Duckworth, S. (1993), *Disability Matters, Seminar Papers*, Tytherley, Salisbury, Disability Matters Ltd.

Employment Department (1993a), *NVQs/SVQs at Higher Levels, A Discussion Paper to the Higher Levels Seminar, October 1992*, Competence and Assessment Briefing Series, Number 8, March 1993, Moorfoot, Sheffield, Employment Department.

Employment Department (1993b), *Prosperity through Skills*, Moorfoot, Sheffield, Employment Department.

Employment Department (1994), *European Communities Branch Audit of European Social Fund, Projects Verification and Audit Section Guide for Applicants*, Research and Development Series, Report No. 17, London, Employment Department.

Employment Department and Department for Education (1995), *Competitiveness, Forging Ahead, Education and Training* (Command 2867), London, ED and DFE.

European Union, Commission for Research, Education, and Training (1995), *Teaching and Learning, Towards the Learning Society, White Paper on Education and Training,* Brussels, CRED.

Evans, N. (1993), Foreword to the series in Field, M., op.cit.

Field, J. (1995), Reality Testing in the Workplace: are NVQs Employment-led?, in Hodkinson, P. & Issitt, M.(eds), op.cit.

Field, M. (1993), *APL, developing more Flexible Colleges,* London, Routledge.

Finn, D. (1995), *Studying while unemployed. The Jobseekers' Allowance and the 16 Hour Rule,* London, Unemployment Unit Briefing.

Frankel, A. (1995a), *Awarding Bodies recognised by the Further Education Funding Council,* Unpublished Paper.

Frankel, A. (1995b), *The Scope and Range of the Further Education Curriculum,* Unpublished Paper.

Further Education Campaign Group (1993), *A New Manifesto for a New Era,* Solihull, FECG.

Further Education Curriculum Review and Development Unit (1981), *Curriculum Control, A review of major styles of curriculum design in FE,* Middlesex, DES and Bristol, Blagdon, FESC.

Further Education Funding Council (1992a), *Funding Learning,* Coventry, FEFC.

Further Education Funding Council (1992b), *Establishment of the FEFC: The membership of the council and the letter of guidance from the Secretary of State for Education,* (Circular 92/08), London, FEFC.

Further Education Funding Council (1993a), *Assessing Achievement,* Coventry, FEFC.

Further Education Funding Council (1993b), *European Social Fund,* Coventry, FEFC.

Further Education Funding Council (1994a), *Disability, Learning Difficulties and Further Eduation, Work in Progress, Professor John Tomlinson, Chairman of the FEFC Committee*, Coventry, FEFC.

Further Education Funding Council (1994b), *General National Vocational Qualifications in the Further Education Sector in England*, Coventry, FEFC.

Further Education Funding Council (1994c), *Guidance on the Recurrent Funding Methodology 1994-1995*, Coventry, FEFC.

Further Education Funding Council (1994d), *How to apply for Recurrent Funding 1995-96*, Coventry, FEFC.

Further Education Funding Council (1994e), *National Vocational Qualifications in the Further Education Sector in England*, Report from the Inspectorate, Coventry, FEFC.

Further Education Funding Council (1995a), *How to apply for funding 1996-97*, Coventry, FEFC.

Further Education Funding Council (1995b), *Recurrent Funding Methodology, Review of the Tariff for 1996-97*, (Circular 95/32), Coventry, FEFC.

Further Education Funding Council (1995c), *FEFC Chief Inspector's Annual Report* (Jan.), Coventry, FEFC.

Further Education Funding Council (1996a), *Analysis of Institutions' Strategic Planning Information*, (Circular 96/02), Coventry, FEFC.

Further Education Funding Council (1996b), *College Responsiveness, National Survey Report from the Inspectorate, Feb 1996*, Coventry, FEFC.

Further Education Funding Council (1996c), *Students' Destinations: College Procedures and Practices*, Coventry, FEFC.

Further Education Funding Council (1996d), *Students with Learning Difficulties and/or Disabilities*, (Circular 96/01), Coventry, FEFC.

Further Education Funding Council (1996e), *Student numbers at colleges in the further education sector in England in 1994-95*, Press Release, 23.1.96, Coventry, FEFC.

Further Education Unit (1981), *Balancing the Equation*, London, FEU.

Further Education Unit (1985a), *Changing the Focus: Women and FE*, London, FEU.

Further Education Unit (1985b), *Curriculum Development for a Multi-cultural Society: Policy and Curriculum*, London, FEU.

Further Education Unit (1987), *FE in Black and White*, York, Longman for FEU.

Further Education Unit (1988), *Staff Development for a Multi-cultural Society*, London, FEU.

Further Education Unit (1989a), *Developing Education and Training Provision for the adult unemployed - a checklist*, London, FEU and REPLAN.

Further Education Unit (1989b), *Ethnic Monitoring in Further and Higher Education*, London, FEU.

Further Education Unit (1992a), *A Basis for Credit*, London, FEU.

Further Education Unit (1992b), *Ethnic Monitoring and its Uses in Colleges*, London, FEU.

Further Education Unit (1994), *Planning, co-ordinating and managing the GNVQ curriculum*, London, FEU.

Further Education Unit and Department of Employment (1992), *Transition into Employment, Developing Competence, Guidelines on implementing provision leading to employment-led qualifications for learners with disabilities and learning difficulties*, London, FEU and DE.

Gleeson, D. (1989), *The Paradox of Training: Making Progress out of crisis*, Milton Keynes, Open University Press.

Glover, L. (ed.) (1995), *GNVQ into practice, how was it for you?* London, Cassell.

Gray, R. (1996), Revolutionary Thoughts, *FE Now*, 2.1996.

Halsey, A.H. (1986), *Change in British Society*, (third edition), Oxford, Oxford University Press.

Harrison, J.F.C. (1954), *A History of The Working Men's College, 1854-1954*, London, Routledge and Kegan Paul.

Heathcote, G., Kempu, R. and Roberts, I. (1982), *Curriculum Styles and Strategies*, London, Further Education Curriculum Review and Development Unit.

HMSO (1944), *Education Act, 1944*, London, HMSO.

HMSO (1956), *White Paper on Technical Education*, London, HMSO.

HMSO (1958), *Training for Skill* (The Carr Report), London, HMSO.

HMSO (1963), *Report of the Committee on Higher Education, appointed by the Prime Minister* (Robbins Report), London, HMSO.

HMSO (1966), *A Plan for Polytechnics and Other Colleges*, White Paper, London, HMSO.

HMSO (1973), *Adult Education: a Plan for Development*, (Russell Report), London, HMSO.

HMSO (1978), *Special Educational Needs, Report of the Committee of Enquiry into the Education of Handicapped Children and Young People*, (Warnock Report), London, HMSO.

HMSO (1988), *Education Reform Act, 1988*, Ch. 40, London, HMSO.

HMSO (1992), *Further and Higher Education Act, 1992*, London, HMSO.

Hodkinson, P. and Issitt, M. (1995), *The Challenge of Competence*, London, Cassell.

Holt, M. (1987), *Skills and Vocationalism, The Easy Answer*, Milton Keynes, Open University Press.

Hutchinson, D. and Tennyson, D. (1986), *Students with Special Needs in FE, a review of current and completed research relating to young people in the 14-19 age range with special educational needs*, Stanmore, Middlesex, FEU and NFER.

Hyland, T. (1994), *Competence, Education and NVQs, dissenting perspectives*, London, Cassell.

Jarvis, P. (1995), *Adult and Continuing Education,* (Second Edition), London, Routledge.

Jenkins, D. and Shipman, M.D. (1976), *Curriculum: an introduction*, London, Open Books.

Johnston, K. (1987), *Exploring the Educational Needs of Unwaged Adults*, Leicester, NIACE and REPLAN.

Kingdon, M. (1991), *The Reform of Advanced Level*, London, Hodder and Stoughton.

Lau-Walker, T. (1995), Further Education and Curriculum in Glover, L (ed.), op.cit.

Lawton, D. (1975), *Class, Culture and the Curriculum*, London, Routledge and Kegan Paul.

Lawton, R. (ed.) (1978), *The Census and Social Structure*, Ilford, Frank Cass.

Lee, G. and Wrench, J. (1983), *Skill Seekers - black youth, apprenticeships and disadvantage*, Leicester, National Youth Bureau.

Lester-Smith, W.O. (1957), *Education, An Introductory Survey*, Harmondsworth, Penguin.

Locke, M. and Pratt, J. (1979), *A Guide to Learning after School*, Harmondsworth, Penguin.

Lowndes, G.A.N. (1961), *The English Educational System*, London, Hutchinson

Maclure, J.S. (1973), *Educational Documents: England and Wales - 1816 to the present day*, London, Methuen.

Mansell, P. (1996a), Could do Better? in *FE Now*, 2.1996.

Mansell, P. (1996b), Must have Recent and Relevant Experience, in *FE Now*, 2.1996.

McCollum, A. and Calder, J. (1995), *Learning Effectiveness of Open and Flexible Learning in Vocational Education*, London, Department for Education and Employment.

McGivney, V. (1990), *Access to Education for Non-Participant Adults*, Leicester, National Institute of Adult Continuing Education.

Ministry of Education (1947), *Further Education: The Scope and Content of its Opportunities under the Education Act, 1944* (Pamphlet Number 8), London, HMSO.

Ministry of Education (1959), *15 to 18, A report of the Central Advisory Council for Education*, Vol 1 (Crowther Report), London, HMSO.

Morris, W. (1890), *News from Nowhere*, in *Three Works by William Morris*, London, Lawrence and Wishart, 1973.

National Advisory Council for Education and Training Targets (NACETT) (1995), *Report on Progress towards the National Targets*, London, NACETT.

National Association for Managers of Student Services in Colleges (1995), *The job seekers allowance....... students under threat?*, NAMSS, internal paper.

National Association of Teachers in Further and Higher Education (NATFHE) (1980), *College Administration, A Handbook*, London, NATFHE.

National Council for Vocational Qualifications (1987a), *Its Purposes and Aims*, London, HMSO.

National Council for Vocational Qualifications (1987b), *The National Vocational Qualification Framework*, London, NCVQ.

National Council for Vocational Qualifications (1988a), *Accreditation Procedures*, London, NCVQ.

National Council for Vocational Qualifications (1988b), *The NVQ Criteria and Related Guidance*, London, NCVQ.

National Council for Vocational Qualifications (1993a), *GNVQ Information Note*, London, NCVQ.

National Council for Vocational Qualifications (1993b), *The Awarding Bodies Common Accord*, London, NCVQ.

National Council for Vocational Qualifications (1994), *Annual Report 1993/4*, London, NCVQ.

Office of Population Censuses and Surveys (1988), *Survey of disability among adults,* Report 1, London, HMSO.

Oliver, M. (1990), *The Politics of Disablement*, Basingstoke, Hampshire, Macmillan.

Payne, J. (1995), *Options at 16 and Outcomes at 24: a Comparision of Academic and Vocational Education and Training Routes*, London, Department for Education and Employment.

Peters, A.J. (1967), *British Further Education*, Oxford, Pergamon.

Pollins, H. (1984), *The History of Ruskin College*, Oxford, Ruskin College Library.

Reeves, F. and colleagues, (1993a), *Community Need and Further Education*, Education Now Books, Ticknall, Derbyshire.

Reeves, F. (1993b), Effects of the 1988 Education Reform Act on Racial Equality of Opportunities in Further Education Colleges in *British Educational Research Journal*, Vol.19, No.3, 1993.

156

Reeves, F. (1995), *The Modernity of Further Education*, Wolverhampton, Bilston College, Education Now.

Roberts, C., Garnett, C., Kapoor, S. and Sarangi, S. (1992), *Quality in teaching and learning. Four multicultural classrooms in Further Education*, London, Department of Employment.

Roberts, M. (1994), *Skills for self-managed learning*, Ticknall, Derbyshire, Education Now.

Robinson, E. (1968), *The New Polytechnics*, Harmondsworth, Penguin.

Robson, M. (1987), *Language Learning and Race, Developing communication skills for a multi-cultural society,* York, Longman for FEU.

Royal Society of Arts Examinations Board (1994), *Well Qualified...Realising Potential...Accounting for Quality....Getting Results*, London, RSA.

Royal Society of Arts (1995), *Annual Report*, London, RSA.

Royle, E. (1987), *Modern Britain, A Social History, 1750 - 1985,* London, Edward Arnold.

Russell, G. J. (1972), *Teaching in Further Education*, London, Pitman Publishing.

Silver, H. and Brennan, J. (1988), *A Liberal Vocationalism*, London, Methuen.

Silver, H. and Teague, S.J. (eds.) (1977), *Chelsea College, a history*, London, University of London, Chelsea College.

Spours, K. (1991), The Politics of Progression in the 14-19 Curriculum, in Chitty , C. (ed.), op.cit.

The Guardian, Education (6.2.96) *Plight of the poor relations.*

Times Educational Supplement, (17.9.93), *Opinion.*

Townsend, C. (1996), Moving with the Times, *FE Now,* New Year, 1996.

Ward, C. (1993), *Systems and Procedures of Certification of Qualifications in the United Kingdom*, London, Employment Department.

Wellington, J. J. (1987), Skills for the Future? in Holt, M., (ed.), op.cit.

West Midlands Travel (1996), *16-18 Photocard Application*, Birmingham, WMT.

Westergaard, J. and Resler, H. (1975), *Class in a Capitalist Society, A Study of Contemporary Britain*, Harmondsworth, Penguin.

Williams, R. (1965), *The Long Revolution*, London, Penguin.

Wren, P. (1995), An introduction to GNVQs, in Glover, L. (ed), op.cit.

Wrench, J. (1986), *YTS, Racial Equality and the Trade Unions, Policy Paper in Ethnic Relations*, No. 6, Warwick, Centre for Research in Ethnic Relations.

Wymer, K. (1995), Open access, partnership, and collaboration, pp. 89-99, in National Institute of Community Education and the College Sector Coalition in association with the Department of Education (1995), *Community Education in South Africa, Conference Report 5-7 July 1995*, South Africa, NICE, CSC and Department of Education.

Young, M.F.D. (ed.) (1971), *Knowledge and Control, New Directions for the Sociology of Education*, London, Collier MacMillan.

Index

curriculum:
convergent invention theory of, 13;
c. cycle, 126;
diffusionist theory of, 13;
dissociative, 4, 11, 14-15, 22, 99, 138;
effectiveness, 110-118;
efficiency, 69-70;
meaning of, 1;
study of, 1-4;
timing of, 3, 5, 88-99;
users of, 3, 5, 37-55.

Dearing Report (16-19), 140-142.
disability, 5, 12, 19, 49-53, 102;
and integration, 51;
Disability Discrimination Act (1955), 53;
statements, 53.
dissociation:
accreditation and provision, 22-3;
curriculum, dissociative, 4, 11, 14 -15, 22, 99, 138.
distance learning, 98;
see also open l.
drop-out, 108.

economy:
and ed., 30-1;
regeneration, 31-2.
Education Act (1944), 7-8, 15, 56-60.
Education Reform Act (1988), 8-9, 61-3.
employers, 4, 112, 123, 139.
empowerment, 36.

English for Speakers of Other Languages, 19, 48-9.
equality of opportunity, 6, 29-30, 47, 121-3.
Europe, 34-6;
Commission for Research Education and Training, 34-6, 122;
culture, 120;
funds, 57, 95-6;
languages, 36.
evening classes, 91.
examinations, 83.
exclusion, 35-6, 122.
expansion of numbers, 37-8, 66, 111.

funding, 66, 93:
census dates, 93;
formula, 62;
funders, 3, 5, 56-71;
learning, 66;
methodology, 24, 53, 65-9, 124, 127.
Further Education Funding Council, 5, 46, 64-5, 70, 81, 113, 128;
funding methodology, 24, 53, 65-9, 93, 124, 127.
Further Education Unit, 46, 79.
Further and Higher Education Act (1992), 9-10, 11, 64-5.
further education:
advanced, 8, 10;
colleges, 10, 64, 65, 91.
definitions, 4, 6-11.
non-advanced, 8.

GCE A level, 7, 24, 73, 84, 87, 94, 120.

BILSTON COLLEGE PUBLICATIONS
Further Education Renaissance Series

Now Available:

Community Need and Further Education by Frank Reeves and colleagues
Specifies the community's educational needs and how they can be met by
describing the practice of community-centred education at Bilston Community
College. (An Education Now Special Report in partnership with
Bilston Community College.) price: £10

The Modernity of Further Education by Frank Reeves
Attempts to describe major developments in colleges and to relate them to more
general theories of social change - or *modernity*. It identifies the general
economic and social forces affecting the lives of people in further education
today and provides an insight into the new further education and the
experience of work and study in the contemporary college.
price: £10

The Further Education Curriculum in England. An Introduction
by Anna Frankel and Frank Reeves
A brief accessible account of the *dissociative or multiform* further education
curriculum: its scope, content, aims, students, funders, providers, accrediting
bodies, modes of attendance, learning methods, and outcomes. price: £9

(While stocks last pack of three, including postage, for £25)

Forthcoming:

Democracy and Further Education by Keith Wymer
Explores the importance of democracy in the governance and management of the further education sector and its colleges. Publication date: June 1996, price: £9

The Further Education Curriculum in England. The Experience
edited by Anna Frankel and Frank Reeves
Following on from their succinct introduction to the further education curriculum, Frankel and Reeves assemble a range of reports and comments from managers, teachers, and students about their experiences of the active college curriculum. Publication date: July 1996, price: £9

Equality of Opportunity in Further Education by Frank Reeves
Defines equality of opportunity in the context of the new further education and explores how it might be achieved. Publication date: October 1996, price: £9

The Quality of Further Education by Anna Frankel
Explains the meaning of quality in relation to further education and provides a critical appraisal of the quality systems available for use in colleges. Publication date: January 1997, price: £9

**Bilston College Publications, Bilston (EO & C) Training Ltd., Bilston Community College, Green Lanes, Wellington Road, Bilston, Wolverhampton, WV14 6EW, England
Tel. no: 01902 821395   Fax. no: 01902 821105**